Date Due

BROWSED		
BROWSED		

Cultures of Mediatization

I

Cultures of Mediatization

Andreas Hepp

Translated by Keith Tribe

polity

First published in German as *Medienkultur. Die Kultur mediatisierter Welten* by Andreas Hepp © Springer VS, Wiesbaden, 2011

This translation copyright © Polity Press 2013

Polity Press
65 Bridge Street
Cambridge CB2 1UR, UK

Polity Press
350 Main Street
Malden, MA 02148, USA

ISBN-13: 978-0-7456-6226-8
ISBN-13: 978-0-7456-6227-5 (pb)

A catalogue record for this book is available from the British Library.

Typeset in 11 on 13 pt Adobe Sabon
by Servis Filmsetting Ltd, Stockport, Cheshire
Printed and bound in Great Britain by the MPG Books Group

The publisher has used its best endeavours to ensure that the URLs for external websites referred to in this book are correct and active at the time of going to press. However, the publisher has no responsibility for the websites and can make no guarantee that a site will remain live or that the content is or will remain appropriate.

Every effort has been made to trace all copyright holders, but if any have been inadvertently overlooked the publisher will be pleased to include any necessary credits in any subsequent reprint or edition.

For further information on Polity, visit our website: www.politybooks.com

Contents

Tables and Figures

Acknowledgements

Each book has a history – this one is no different. The first ideas for this volume go back to conversations with various colleagues around 2004 and 2005 who expressed the need for a book about present media cultures. The initial outlines were written in various versions; different chapters had been planned as part of this book but were eventually published as articles. The reason for this is that the concept for the text underwent change while it was still being formulated: more and more, it became obvious that the original idea to write an all-embracing monograph on media cultures in their various forms is at present an impossible undertaking. This is because we need far more research to be able to write such a book. Therefore, we need something completely different, i.e. an outline of the concepts and theoretical points of departure requisite for such analyses. The present book on *Cultures of Mediatization* is my attempt to do this.

Cultures of Mediatization is based on very different experiences. First of all, I want to mention the MA programme in Media Culture at the University of Bremen. Its various student projects analyse countless moments of media cultures. In my project-orientated teaching, I became increasingly aware that the most important question revolves around how we can study these moments of media culture in a way that enables the integration of such analyses. Second, I have to make mention of the cooperative and very collegial research at the ZeMKI (Centre in Media, Communication and Information Research) at the University of

Acknowledgements

Bremen on questions of the mediatization of culture in the context of eventization, migration, mobility and politics. This research demonstrated how far we are from an all-inclusive description of media cultures. At the same time, it indicates how necessary more integrative concepts and theoretizations are. And, third, there is the priority research programme, 'Mediatized Worlds', being developed by Friedrich Krotz, Christiane Funken, Michael Jäckel and myself and funded by the German Research Foundation (DFG). This programme offers the space for an empirically based theoretization and conceptualization of mediatization.

This short description of the context in which *Cultures of Mediatization* has been written shows that the book owes a lot to a great number of people. First of all, this includes Friedrich Krotz, with whom I have had the chance to increasingly deepen our collaborative research on mediatization over recent years. Much of this book draws on contributions made by my colleagues at the ZeMKI, who have accompanied me for many years in the course of my empirical research on media culture: Andreas Breiter, who gave me many hints on questions of technology; Marco Höhn, with whom I had the chance to discuss various questions of youth scenes; Veronika Krönert, who together with me researched the mediatization of religion; Cigdem Bozdag and Laura Suna, who were involved with me in a project on the mediatization of diasporas; Michael Brüggemann, Katharina Kleinen-von Königslöw, Swantje Lingenberg, Anke Offerhaus and Johanna Möller, with whom I have analysed political discourse cultures in Europe; Matthias Berg and Cindy Roitsch, with whom I am at present working on the mediatization of communitization. This cooperative research has formed a very important basis for the present book. Last but not least, throughout my time at the University of Bremen my research has been greatly supported by Heide Pawlik.

As important as the foregoing are the many encounters, talks and discussions with friends and colleagues. Especially, I wish to thank Nick Couldry, Jostein Gripsrud, Maren Hartmann, Uwe Hasebrink, Ronald Hitzler, Hubert Knoblauch, Sonia Livingstone, Knut Lundby, Shaun Moores, Michaela Pfadenhauer, Jo Reichertz, Kevin Robins, Waldemar Vogelgesang, Gerhard Vowe and Jeffrey

Acknowledgements

Wimmer – and the many anonymous reviewers of conferences and journals who gave me important feedback while developing the ideas in this volume. For the feedback on different chapters of this book I want to thank Nick Couldry, Ronald Hitzler, Friedrich Krotz, Jo Reichertz and the members of my research group (Bora Aksen, Matthias Berg, Cigdem Bozdag, Monika Elsler, Julia Gantenberg, Sigrid Kannengießer, Swantje Lingenberg, Anne Mollen, Johanna Möller, Annalena Oeffner, Anke Offerhaus, Cindy Roitsch and Laura Suna). I want to thank *Communications: The European Journal for Communication Research* for permission to include Chapter 3, which is revised version of the article originally published as 'Mediatization and the "Molding Force" of the Media', in *Communications* 37(1), 2012, pp. 1–28, DOI: 10.1515/commun-2012-001. Monika Elsler, Heide Pawlik and Judith Niesel supported me with proofs and organizational help. I also want to thank Barbara Emig-Roller from VS Verlag for her great editorial help and Andrea Drugan from Polity Press for magnificent support as editor. Also many thanks to Keith Tribe, who translated the German edition of 'Cultures of Mediatization'. From him I learned that translation means reworking to make an argument work in a completely different language context. I am also very thankful to Justin Dyer for his careful and supportive copy-editing.

But especially I want to thank my family – Beate Köhler, Levi and Naomi Hepp – who gave me the space to write this book and without whom it would not have been possible.

1

Introduction

Why should anyone today write a book about media culture? For a book with a title like this one, we should certainly ask this question right away, and this 'why?' has at least two aspects. First of all, it can be asked why one is still preoccupied by the *topic* of media culture. For decades there has been academic discussion of the degree to which our contemporary cultures are to be regarded as media cultures. Moreover, in our newspapers and magazines we also find discussion of tendencies of development, decline and change in our media cultures. Secondly, it can be asked why such discussion should take the *form* of a book. Today's media culture is of course increasingly digitalized, and the Internet is the dominating environment. I would like to respond to both questions at the beginning of this book.

The reason for dealing with the *topic* of media culture lies in the fact that, since the very first writings on modern mass culture and the influence of the media, ever more has been written and published about media culture. However, the analyses that have resulted are, I believe, inadequate for a proper appraisal of the ongoing transition of our culture into a media culture. This is because the significance of this transition is underrated, lacking sufficient understanding of the way in which the media – or, more exactly, communication via media – have increasingly left their mark on our everyday life, our identity and the way in which we live together. *Media* communication appears in such discussion as to some extent merely secondary. By contrast we can read pieces in which media are talked up into the essence of change and transition – that we are leaving the era of the book or of the television and entering the bright new world of the Internet. A basic argument that will be developed in the course of this book is that both these ways of thinking about media culture are misguided. If we would really like to know how our culture has been and is being transformed into a media culture through the increasing use of media, then we need a much more complex approach than either of these extremes, so that we might avoid simplified argument. Media cultures are cultures of mediatization: that is, cultures that are 'moulded' by the media.

And here we can start to see why this should be presented in the form of a book. Some years ago now, in his historical study *In the Vineyard of the Text* (1993), the philosopher and theologian Ivan Illich examined the early development of the modern book, in the course of which he reflected that, as he wrote this book, the form of communication that it represented was threatened with decline. Time has passed since then, and the book as a form of communication is still here. Despite all the dire predictions, even the Internet has changed nothing. In fact, the Internet has become a platform for the purchase of printed books from websites as well as for downloading digital books. The actual non-disappearance of the book as a communicative form indicates that it has properties and possibilities that no Internet encyclopaedia, blog or article in an online academic journal has: the book makes it possible to develop an overarching argument through many pages, an argument that cannot be reduced to a few bullet points. Since an investigation of media culture involves wide-ranging questions affecting everybody, and not only academics interested in communication and the media, answers to these questions cannot be reduced to a few Wikipedia entries, for all one's sympathy with online reference sources. That is why my discussion and argument are presented in the form of a book. My hope in publishing in this form is that the book is interesting and readable, stimulating readers to develop a different way of dealing with media in everyday life.

But before I go any further, it is important to introduce and clarify three basic concepts, so that later misunderstanding might be avoided: the concepts of communication, medium and culture.

If I refer to *communication*, I mean any form of symbolic inter-action conducted either in a planned and conscious manner or in a highly habituated and socially situated way (Reichertz 2009: 94). Communication therefore involves the use of signs that humans learn during their socialization and which, as symbols, are for the most part entirely arbitrary, depending for their meaning upon conventionalized social rules. There is no 'natural reason' for calling a tree 'tree'. Interaction means people's reciprocally related social action. This implies that humans 'do something' in orienta-tion with each other. Communication is fundamental to the human construction of reality: that is, we ourselves 'create' our social reality in multiple communicative processes. We are born into a world in which communication already exists; we learn what is characteristic of this world (and its culture) through the (com-municative) process of learning to speak; and when we proceed to act in this world our action is always also communicative action. Many theorists have discussed these issues (for an overview see Krotz 2008a). Peter Berger and Thomas Luckmann, whose work *The Social Construction of Reality* (1967) became a sociological classic, formulated this as follows: 'The most important vehicle of reality-maintenance is conversation. One may view the individual's everyday life in terms of the working away of a conversational apparatus that ongoingly maintains, modifies and reconstructs his subjective reality' (Berger and Luckmann 1967: 172). It would be hard to find a more striking and precise way of describing the con-stitutive force of communication for our human reality as so many of these forms of communication are today mediated by media.

Which brings us to the concept of *medium*. Wherever in the following I refer to a medium, I mean a given technological com-munication medium. I am not concerned with the general symbolic media discussed in sociological systems theory, such as power, money and love (which, in regard to my later usage, have also been confusingly called 'media of communication', see Luhmann 1997: 316ff.). Nor am I interested in language (or our bodies) as a 'primary medium' (Beth and Pross 1976: 112–19) based upon

3

the 'biological organization' of humans (Elias 1991: 23). My use of 'media' adheres quite closely to its everyday meaning: the set of institutions and technical apparata that we humans employ to communicate across space and time. Important here is that technical media of *communication* are at issue, those media that the informational theorist and organizational analyst Herbert Kubicek has called 'second-order media' (1997). For Kubicek, 'first-order media' are technological systems with particular functions and potentialities for the dissemination of information in the technical sense of the word: for instance, the Internet as a vehicle for the Transmission Control Protocol/Internet Protocol (TCP/IP) model. 'Second-order media' are in addition socio-cultural institutions of communication. This would be, for example, not the Internet itself but an online newspaper or email. And so when reference is made to 'media' in the following this means 'second-order media' media of this kind. This is a technical means of mediating communication involving (at minimum) a technically based system of signs embedded in a particular social institutional structure, and which as such facilitates communicative action (Beck 2006: 14).

The most complex concept used in this book is certainly that of *culture*, or media culture. Ultimately the entire book deals with the question of what media culture is. Without wishing to anticipate the arguments that I present, it nonetheless seems necessary to make some preliminary remarks about this, so that we do not get sidetracked from the very beginning. First of all, I use the expression 'culture', or 'media culture', in the singular when seeking to establish the term as a concept. Of course, I do not assume that there is only one (media) culture: from the empirical point of view there is only a plurality of cultures. In addition to that it has to be taken into account that cultures are formed at very different levels. A few years ago the German writer Eckhard Henscheid wrote a book with the title *All 756 Cultures: An Assessment* (2001). In what he referred to as a 'Grand Prix for cultures' he demonstrated the presence of 756 different ways of using the expression 'culture' in everyday German language. These run from A (*abendländischer Kultur* – occidental culture) to Z (*Zynismuskultur* – culture of cynicism). The book can be used as proof of the fact that there

4

is not simply a 'national culture' (which Henscheid refers to as 'German culture'), but multifarious cultures. I would like to take up this idea, although I would also wish to render it more precise than a simple additive approach can. Culture is always to do with the production of everyday meanings. Borrowing from Stuart Hall (1997: 222), we can understand by 'culture' the 'sum of the different classificatory systems and discursive formations' to which our production of everyday meanings relates. Systems of classification are ultimately the pattern of systematic relationships between signs (understanding 'sign' in a very broad sense, and not only as a linguistic sign). Discursive formations are continuing patterned and power-producing constellations of the use of these signs in linguistic and non-linguistic practice. Culture is always a matter of practice, the 'doing' part of the production of meanings. Hence culture is thoroughly contradictory and embedded in a process of social contestation and discussion. Questions of culture are likewise questions of power: whoever is able to define what 'culture' is and is not holds power. German discussion of a 'primary culture' (*Leitkultur*) is a clear example of this. What is important is to keep in mind that we live simultaneously in a number of cultures. These are not simply the given national cultures, but also 'democratic cultures', 'protest cultures', 'musical cultures', to cite some examples from Eckhard Henscheid's collection. We can take their sheer multiplicity as an indication that cultures flow into and over each other; they are not that well defined and are best conceived as 'thickenings'.

These points regarding the concept of culture already suggest how many-layered the phenomenon of media culture as 'cultures of mediatization' is. To deal with this we need to work with all three concepts – communication, medium and culture – and not seek to further differentiate them. Above all we need to see the connections between them. For I would in this book like to show that media cultures are those cultures whose primary resources are mediated by technological means of communication, and in this process are 'moulded' in various ways that must be carefully specified. That is the reason why I call them 'cultures of mediatization'.

The line of argument that I would like to develop in this book runs as follows. I begin in Chapter 2 with a review of the existing theory and analysis of media culture. I will argue that these approaches do shed light upon important aspects of media culture, but they do not really provide anything in the way of an adequate point of departure for theoretically founded and empirically informed research into media culture. Hence, following such a critique, one must seek to construct a suitable point of departure step by step. This begins with the definition of mediatization as a metaprocess and panorama (Chapter 3), a definition which seeks a line of demarcation with respect to concepts of mediation (*Vermittlung*) and media logic. This conceptual work then allows us to develop in Chapter 4 an understanding of media culture which conceives this as cultures of mediatization. Useful concepts for the description of media cultures will here be found in the ideas of mediatized worlds, communication networks and communicative figuration. Chapter 5 then follows by raising an important aspect of today's media cultures: how we live in different forms of translocal communities. Finally, Chapter 6 deals with the question of what might be an appropriate methodological approach for the empirical study of media cultures. The book is concluded in Chapter 7, where I seek to formulate some thoughts on how, given the account of media cultures and their change which I have developed, further questions and criticism might be integrated.

This outline already makes clear that this book is no final description of what media cultures are today. It is more of a draft, an appeal, a sketch which seeks to grasp what we need to consider if we wish properly to comprehend ongoing cultural change. It is in this sense, then, that this book is intended to prompt further questions and research, rather than premature answers.

2

What Media Culture Is (Not)

As already noted in the Introduction, media culture has for a long time been a topic for research in the study of communication and media. This has not, however, prevented the development of many misconceptions about what exactly media culture is, misconceptions that have been formed on the basis of different approaches and strands of thought. In this chapter I seek to deal with what I consider to be the most prominent misconceptions commonly encountered in everyday discussions of the media. And to make myself quite clear from the outset: media culture is neither a mass culture, nor the culture of a particular dominating medium (whether books, TV or the world-wide web); nor is it a programme that integrates us into one society, or a cyberculture that gradually enmeshes us and turns us into cyborgs or cyberpunks. But we cannot simply dismiss out of hand the way in which various discourses mobilize these and other concepts in their construction of what media culture is supposed to be. Even if particular conclusions seem to be wrong, or at least problematic, they do nonetheless conceal ideas with whose help we can learn something of what media culture really is. And so this chapter represents a second step in a gradual approach to an understanding of the real nature of media culture.

Omnipresent, But Not a Mass Culture

If one asks where we can find the very first reflections about media culture, sooner or later we come across Critical Theory, as practised by the Frankfurt School. This is a form of critical sociology developed by members of the Institut für Sozialforschung, which opened its doors in Frankfurt am Main in 1924. The most important representatives of this School are generally thought to be Max Horkheimer, Director of the Institut for many years, and Theodor Adorno. From the late 1930s to the mid-1940s, while in American exile, they worked together on their well-known book *Dialectic of Enlightenment* (1947). The concept which this book placed centre stage was not that of media culture, but rather the culture industry and its mass culture.

In their book Adorno and Horkheimer describe the culture industry as an omnipresent system. This culture industry is said to be a 'filter' through which the whole world passes (Horkheimer and Adorno 1986: 126). The term 'culture industry' is intended to make plain that this is not a culture spontaneously formed among the masses, the contemporary form of popular art. The central characteristic of the culture industry is standardization and serialization: 'procedural schematization' (Horkheimer and Adorno 1986: 136), the 'constant reproduction of the same thing' (Horkheimer and Adorno 1986: 134). The production of cultural commodities proceeds according to standardized patterns, their content deriving from the same common model – whether of genre, narrative or staging. The constant industrial dynamic of innovation lies in the variation of these patterns. And we can add to the elements of the culture industry described by Adorno and Horkheimer not only culture as commodity, but also the apparatus of production, the culture market and cultural consumption (Müller-Doohm 2008).

The commodities produced by the culture industry – for Adorno and Horkheimer the genre films of the 1940s were an obvious example – are of such a nature that consumers are rendered passive when confronted with the superficial activity of constantly changing images whose substance nonetheless remains unchanged;

and this passivity immobilizes consumers' 'thinking activity' (Horkheimer and Adorno 1986: 126–7). The consequence of the standardization of products is a standardization of reception and a 'pseudo-individuality' of people. The life of one's own individuality comes to depend on the acquisition of normalized media contents – as for example in the cultural model presented by the life of the stars – and these become the all-enveloping basis of the articulation of one's own identity. The entertainment provided by the culture industry is therefore a standardized enjoyment. Correspondingly, the enjoyment offered by the culture industry represents a flight – not a flight from an evil reality, but rather from any thought of resistance (Horkheimer and Adorno 1986: 144). This is a standardized 'mass culture' (Adorno 1975: 12; Horkheimer and Adorno 1986: 152). Hence the total effect of the culture industry is that of an anti-Enlightenment:

> But what is new is that the irreconcilable elements of culture, art and distraction, are subordinated to one end and subsumed under one false formula: the totality of the culture industry. It consists of repetition. That its characteristic innovations are never anything more than improvements of mass reproduction is not external to the system. It is with good reason that the interest of innumerable consumers is directed to the technique, and not to the contents – which are stubbornly repeated, outworn, and by now half-discredited. The social power which the spectators worship shows itself more effectively in the omnipresence of the stereotype imposed by technical skill than in the stale ideologies for which the ephemeral contents stand in. (Horkheimer and Adorno 1986: 136)

Their vision of the culture industry and its mass culture is a very gloomy one, possibly one about which we would today have distinct reservations, a vision which now seems in some aspects at least a reflection of their experience of fascism and American exile. All the same, if we adopt a rather different perspective, Adorno and Horkheimer's theory of the culture industry does have relevance to what we might today call media culture: they were among the first to point to a phenomenon that we might today call the *omnipresence of media culture*. Penetration of the entire society by the culture industry is a matter concerning not just the production of cultural commodities and the production process itself, but also the identities with which people live: 'The whole world is made to pass through the filter of the culture industry' (Horkheimer and Adorno 1986: 126).

If we take a quotation like this, it is in fact possible to read Adorno and Horkheimer's arguments rather differently. The theory of the culture industry becomes an early attempt at critical reflection on the ubiquity of media communication in the modern world. That there is a direct line connecting the theory of the culture industry to new approaches to the description of media culture should not be any surprise. A prominent example of this is the work of Douglas Kellner, which connects directly to the Frankfurt School, but also to contemporary cultural studies (Kellner 1995a). The way in which Kellner develops his concept of media culture takes up aspects of the culture industry theory: for him, media culture is above all a culture generated by (mass) media and the culture industry. However, for Kellner, media culture cannot be detached from people's lives: society and culture are 'colonized by media culture', 'media culture has come to dominate everyday life, serving as the ubiquitous background and often the highly seductive foreground of our attention and activity . . .' (Kellner 1995b: 3). Here too we find the idea of the omnipresence of media culture, an idea developed directly from Critical Theory. Of course, Kellner regards media culture with a much greater degree of ambivalence than did Adorno and Horkheimer when confronted with mass culture, for he maintains that while 'media culture . . . induces individuals to conform to the established organization of society . . . it also provides resources that can empower individuals against that society' (Kellner 1995b: 3).

Kellner thus gives us something to reflect on here. He argues that media cultures are extremely complex phenomena which have so far evaded adequate theorization, in spite of the many attempts made at developing such approaches. As he says, most of the *general* theories of media culture seem merely one-sided and blind to its important features and complexities. He therefore proposes that theories of media culture are best developed from the analysis of concrete phenomena in their historical and social context. Even if this book does not follow Kellner's proposition and instead presents some general points about media culture, his approach has to be taken seriously.

But let us go back to the arguments advanced by Adorno and Horkheimer. Placed in the context of later discussion of media culture, their cultural pessimism lacks empirical foundation, and certainly represents a very limited perspective. Media culture is not simply a mass, standardized culture, but is much more contradictory and open than Adorno and Horkheimer allow. Kellner has pointed this out, as have many others (see, for example, Negus 2006). But there is another point on which Adorno and Horkheimer's perspective has been positively influential in work on media culture. Very early on they identified the importance of what can be called the omnipresence of media culture. This means that any reflection on media culture cannot just be based on the idea that media culture is the culture represented in the media – and so TV culture in the sense of TV broadcasting, or film culture in the sense of the culture represented in films, and so on. Comprehending media culture is a much more complex enterprise, since our entire construction of reality is increasingly effected through communication which, at least *in part*, is conveyed through media. This is what we have to address, and it has always proved a major challenge for any attempt to define what media culture really is.

Marked by the Medium, But Not Dominated by One Medium

The search for a suitable concept of media culture leads not only to the Frankfurt School, but also to so-called 'Medium Theory'. This is an approach first developed during the 1950s at the University of Toronto, very much influenced by the work of the (cultural) economist Harold Innis and, later, the communications theorist Marshall McLuhan. For Joshua Meyrowitz, currently one of the leading representatives of Medium Theory and author of the book *No Sense of Place* (1987), this approach can provide an alternative basis for understanding the impact of media. Medium Theory presupposes that, if we are to properly appreciate the potential effects of media, we need to shift our attention away from a focus on media contents as the primary source of media effect, and instead 'look to the nature and capacities of each medium itself' (Meyrowitz 2009: 518). This perspective combines the varied work of Medium Theory, linking high-level macro questions concerning long-term processes of change (Innis 1950, 1951; McLuhan 1962; Ong 2002) to the results of micro studies of the manner in which people's interactional relations are modified through media (Meyrowitz 1987).

For our present discussion of media culture we are first of all interested in what Meyrowitz calls the macro approaches of the first generation of Medium Theorists, which can also be found in other recent writings (cf. Poe 2011). The changes in media culture are set out by these theorists as a sequence of different cultures, each of which is characterized by a dominant medium (for a survey of this see Meyrowitz 1995). *Traditional oral cultures* construct their memory through a purely oral mode of communication, using rhythmic poems and simple mythic narration. Since the oral nature of these cultures requires the physical presence of those involved in the communicative process, there is in such cultures a natural limit to communicative contact, its extent and its complexity. *Written cultures*, in which there is knowledge of a written language, are clearly demarcated from oral cultures. Writing not only makes it possible to communicate across time and space; it also makes it possible to compose longer and more complex texts. Writing is therefore a condition for the emergence of philosophy, literature and science. However, composition of such work presupposed that there were experts in written discourse, and this led to an increasing inequality within societies based upon a written culture. Meyrowitz sums this up as follows: 'The impact of writing, therefore, is uneven until the development of the printing press in the fifteenth century, the spread of schooling, and the corresponding growth of literacy form the sixteenth to the nineteenth century' (1995: 55). In this perspective the emergence of modern Europe

12

coincides with the 'rise of modern print culture' (Meyrowitz 1995: 55). From the point of view of Medium Theory this *modern print culture* corresponds to the establishment of different informational worlds: even if compulsory schooling later generalized literacy, the informational worlds of 'well-read' experts shifted away from other sections of the population. At the same time the printing of books first made possible the formation of large, integrated political unities, since the potential for 'massed' communication in turn made possible the communicative inclusion of broader sections of the population. In general, however, for Medium Theory it was a change in thinking that was the principal outcome: the printed book facilitated not only the idea of authorship and intellectual property, but also the widespread institutionalization of science – the university as a place of study in its modern sense emerged. The spread of literacy and of the printed book also implied a growing equality among communicative partners, an equality which, together with the increased value placed upon 'scientific knowledge', led to the rejection of traditional forms of rule. The Reformation is an early example of this.

A *global electronic culture* developed from this, according to Medium Theory. This is the phase in which different forms of electronic media become established: first the telegraph, then the telephone, radio, TV, later on various Internet media and mobile communications. Medium Theory argues that these electronic media recapitulate features of oral culture: 'simultaneity of action, perception, and reaction' (Meyrowitz 1995: 57). As Walter Ong has emphasized in his text *Orality and Literacy* (2002), this involves a 'secondary orality', one which is based upon writing and the possibility of (electronic) reproduction. For example, if discussion on TV is presented live and as speech, this still depends upon prior written formulations. And much of real-time Internet communication is written: email and chatrooms are only the most obvious example. Representatives of Medium Theory treat these developments as follows:

New forms of concrete sensory experience compete with abstract print knowledge. And the word returns in its old form – as an event rather than as an object. But the scale of sharing is far different. Electronic media are like extensions of our sensory apparatus that reach around the planet. Electronic sensors return us to seemingly 'direct' encounters, but on a global scale.

As a result of the widespread use of electronic media, there is a greater sense of personal involvement with those who would otherwise be strangers – or enemies. The seemingly direct experience of distant events by average citizens fosters a decline in print-supported notions of delegated authority, weakening the power of political parties, unions and government bureaucracies. The sharing of experience across nations dilutes the power of the nation state. (Meyrowitz 1995: 58)

There are clear echoes here of Marshall McLuhan's conception of a 'global village' (1962: 293), once thought to be an extremely visionary conception of a world-wide neighbourhood based upon electronic media. According to Meyrowitz, the task of the second generation of Medium Theorists is to reinforce the existing conception of a four-phase development of media cultures, a rough outline framing the transformation of media and culture, adding to that detailed analysis of changes in relationships of interaction. Changes in media do not therefore have a direct impact upon everyday life; rather this process of change alters informational networks, role relationships and human group identities. This can be said for each of the four main phases, whether these are traditional oral cultures, written cultures, print cultures or electronic cultures – in each of these informational networks, role relationships and human group identities were quite differently structured.

Medium Theory is not alone in putting forward a conception of the cultural history of humankind in terms of a sequence of dominant media. Niklas Luhmann, for instance, has described the transition in societies in terms of the emergence of 'media of dissemination', to use his words (1997: Vol. 1, 202–315). He suggests that language, writing, the printed book and electronic media here play a moulding and leading role. Of greater interest, however, are the older writings of the cultural sociologist Friedrich Tenbruck, since these are much closer to the work of connectivity theorists today. Tenbruck identifies three ideal types of society on the basis of the social differentiation arising from the human division of labour: oral society, high culture and modern society. He places much greater emphasis than Medium Theory does on the question of locality and translocal connectivity arising out of technical media (or the formation of networks). He argues that *oral societies*, differentiated only by age, are based upon local groups whose members stand in a relationship of direct contact with one another in the here and now. *High cultures* are characterized by the division of labour and a differentiation of higher and lower strata, and imply a translocal ruling apparatus which, to function, needs the possibilities offered by translocal communication. Media-based interaction using writing permits the construction and maintenance of an apparatus of rule through the creation of a 'super-local communicative network' (Tenbruck 1972: 59). This pulls diverse localities together into a network and makes possible the identification of local groups as part of larger communities – here religion plays an especially important role. Nonetheless, the prospects of greater and more comprehensive communicative integration are limited. *Modern societies*, characterized by more extensive social differentiation, while also 'abolishing the important difference for high culture between an upper stratum and local elements' (Tenbruck 1972: 64), suggest the importance of mass media, which, as means of communication, 'bring together members of society, independent of their locality, into ever new, often transitory and passive groups, in this way putting them in touch with the onward movement of society' (Tenbruck 1972: 66).

As these examples show, the propositions of Medium Theory should not be treated in isolation, for they indicate the existence of a broad stream of thinking in the social and cultural sciences, especially in cultural sociology. This focus upon particular (ideal) types of cultures or societies in this approach is certainly very attractive: we can conceive the specificity of a culture and society in terms of a dominant medium. And as these dominating media change, then so do the forms of culture and society. *Media culture is thus a culture characterized by a specific dominating medium – and this is, according to methodological preference, an ideal or a real type.*

But on further reflection one becomes ambivalent about Medium Theory and similar approaches. On the one hand, the idea that media are not neutral and have very wide-ranging effects upon the character of our cultures and societies is a very attractive one. Treating Medium Theory as '[a]n alternative to the dominant paradigm of media effects' (Meyrowitz 2009: 517) is extremely productive for the discussion engaged here. This approach insists that it is often not so much a specific content which has an 'impact' upon culture and society. It seems more relevant to consider how media as such generate their effects, understanding by media here a complex of institutionalized and reified communicative arrangements (Meyrowitz 2009: 518–20). This in turn opens our eyes to the way in which we have to understand cultures as specifically moulded by media; and this process of moulding is something that must be studied empirically across different media cultures. In this sense Medium Theory is a basis for what Theo Hug and Norm Friesen (2009) call the 'mediatic turn' – a 'turn' to the mediality of communication: that is to say, the ecological and material character as means of communication (see also Schofield Clark 2009).

But on the other hand Medium Theory leaves the impression of being an inadequate approach to the description of media culture, precisely *because* it reduces this media culture to that of one dominant media culture. One medium (speech, writing, the book) is treated as the given dominating force in a culture, something which is the primary structuring element of communication in that culture. But this is too simplistic: cultures moulded by media are much too contradictory to be reduced to any one dominating medium. Medium Theory, for example, treats the present as a global culture of electronic media, but then has trouble identifying *one* particular dominant and leading medium, clearly showing that socio-cultural change is too varied to be reduced to any one leading medium. Globalized, mostly text-based Internet communication is as much a part of today's cultures as is the visual communication of high-definition TV (HDTV) and event cinema. Political campaigns are, for instance, organized simultaneously through the Internet, TV and cinema:

using email or related advertising through the social web to build support; using live reports on and images from campaign events in HDTV; and creating costly documentary versions that can be treated as events in themselves. One example of this is the involvement in environmental protection of Al Gore, the American politician and winner of the Nobel Peace Prize (see on this Dörner 2006).

This argument can also be developed historically, as is demonstrated by studies in media history. Hence, for example, Medium Theory clearly overestimates the revolutionary impact of printing, since, following its advent, various forms of oral communication retained their (public) value. Besides dialogue as a way of teaching in schools and universities, it can be shown in respect of the Reformation that the diffusion of Luther's writings was closely related to his activities as a public speaker. Historical studies reveal that Luther was above all very effective in direct communication, and in spreading his ideas and principles he relied mainly on direct speech (Bösch 2011: 49–57).

It is therefore less the *individual* dominant medium that defines media cultures, but *extremely complex arrangements of different forms of media-based, communicative action*. It is these that have to be described if we wish to understand the specificities of media cultures.

Constitutive of Reality, But No Integrative Programme

There is another approach to communication and media with a very particular approach to the nature of media culture: radical constructivism, which is particularly widespread in German-language research and which originated in the early 1980s. This approach spread beyond academia through the educational radio series broadcast in 1990–1 by Hessische Rundfunk entitled *Media and Communication*, intended by its producers as part of the station's programme of general continuing education (see for a discussion of its study materials Merten et al. 1994). The leading representative of radical constructivism is Siegfried J. Schmidt, whose publications have had a lasting impact upon the development of radical constructivism.

There is a general sense in which those approaches to media culture already discussed are also constructivist in tenor: they do not treat media culture – whether conceived as a mass culture, or as a culture characterized by a dominant medium – as a simple 'given'. Media culture is understood as something 'made' by people, and is therefore in this sense constructed. However, *radical* constructivism presents a 'radicalized' version of social constructivism since it 'supplements' (Schmidt 1994a: 6) it with material drawn from neuroscience and cognitive science, while integrating this with a functionalist system-theoretical perspective upon media culture – this was how Schmidt presented it in the course of his writings. His point of departure is, however, different from that of Niklas Luhmann, the leading German representative of systems theory. For Luhmann, communication is the basis of social systems, and so his arguments exclude any orientation to the actor; radical constructivists set out from the individual actor as a closed cognitive system and on this basis develop a social theory. The epistemological foundations of this take the following form, Schmidt here referring not only to Luhmann but also to Gerhard Roth, the biologist and cognitive scientist:

> Today there is consensus both across constructivist-biological (G. Roth) and differential logic (N. Luhmann) approaches to theories of epistemology and cognition that human perception of the environment is not a representational process, but one of construction. Perception is work done by the observer on differences and distinctions encountered in the human environment, in which it cannot be ascertained whether or not these differences originate in this environment. . . . Our evaluation of what we consciously treat as knowledge is not done through a comparison with 'reality', but is achieved through action and communication. Knowledge is therefore checked against other knowledge that we have gained through action and communication. We accept that which is viable, workable and successful, not that which is (ontologically) true. In other words, one construction of reality is validated by other constructions of reality. (Schmidt 1992: 429–3)

18

On this basis Schmidt has developed a theory of media culture. In his understanding, culture is, together with cognition, media and communication, one of four instances in the circular process of the construction of reality (Schmidt 2000: 98). He is critical of the way in which the various concepts of culture already established in the humanities and social sciences – beginning with the ethnological conception of culture, passing through cultural semiotics, cultural sociology and culture and personality research – implicitly or explicitly involve an opposition of nature to culture. Schmidt considers this kind of understanding of culture to be problematic since it rules out any possible interchange between human biological evolution ('nature') and the formation of culture (Schmidt 1994b: 217).

Instead he takes James R. Beniger's concept of 'cultural programming' (Beniger 1986: 61) and uses it to develop a different approach. For Beniger, DNA is genetically programmed, organizations are programmed by formal procedures and decision rules, mechanical and electronic processes are programmed by algorithms; but the brain is culturally programmed. This 'cultural programme', which ultimately maintains (social) control and hence integration, is conveyed to humans in their socialization. From this perspective, then, cultural programming 'is decisive for any society that is based upon the co-operation of individuals *qua* individuals' (Schmidt 1994b: 225). Control results here not from a causal relationship, but from culturally programmed meaning. This conception of control through cultural programming does not exclude individual creativity, but is implicitly accepted in all individual action. On this basis Schmidt then develops a conception of 'culture as a programme' which emphasizes the processual aspect – in contrast to the idea of 'culture as a system' rather than a structure, like the 'dynamic cultural sociology' of Walter L. Bühl (1986: 124):

> I accordingly conceptualize culture . . . as a programme, in the sense of a limited number of specific rules or principles, permitting the creation of a large number of individual events. This programme is . . . dynamic and has a learning capacity, also permitting subprogrammes

19

to be created for particular purposes. Culture can be conceptualized, in the non-substantial sense advanced here, as a programme for the implementation of sociality at the levels of cognition, communication and social structure. (Schmidt 1994b: 242–3)

Hence culture specifies which meaningful distinctions constitute social systems. In this approach social systems are inconceivable in the absence of cultural programmes, since the implementation of sociality presupposes a programme that is followed collectively, through which cognitive expectations, symbolic communicative forms together with political, religious, economic and other institutions are checked and controlled intersubjectively (cf. Schmidt 1994b: 234). The openness, and the capacity to learn and reflect, which characterizes such programmes varies from society to society. This in turn suggests the necessity of treating culture as an integrative all-embracing programme which embodies the communicative intersection of any one (national) society's model of reality.

Schmidt develops his conception of *media culture* on this basis of this understanding of culture. This is derived from the connection that he posits between cognition, media, communication and culture in the circular process of the construction of reality. In this context media have valency because it is through them that processes of communication are set in motion. Media outputs are therefore the central element connecting cognition (the psychic system) and communication (the basis of the social system). Cognitive operations have to be transformed into particular media outputs to initiate communication, while media outputs are then transformed into cognitive operations so that new communication can be facilitated. In short, according to Schmidt, cognition and communication each work within distinct and autonomous systems. Media outputs link up these systems, motivating system-specific construction processes.

This line of argument gains some traction once we place it in the context of the differentiation of modern society into various functional systems, such as politics, economy, the sciences, and so forth. According to the radical constructivists, the various func-

20

tional systems of modern society are synchronized through mass media. These have developed into an autonomous social system that represents the 'global media system' of a (national) society (Schmidt 1992: 440; cf. also Luhmann 2000). Such systems – according to Schmidt, but who here argues in a way similar to Werner Faulstich (1998) – have increasingly assumed the role within functionally differentiated societies of forming a model of reality accessible to all, offering an authentic feeling of being a part of that society; and this occurs, in Schmidt's words, through the 'staging of realities' (1992: 440).

Taking full account of the implications of this position, Schmidt maintains that culture in functionally differentiated societies can only be treated as media culture. If we conceive culture in the sense outlined above as 'the socially binding and historically reproduced programme for the synchronization of individually formed constructions of reality' (Schmidt 2000: 41), and at the same time assume that in functionally differentiated societies the mass media have become the central instance of these social reproduction processes, then culture in functionally differentiated societies is manifested as media culture (cf. Schmidt 1992: 440f.). However, this should not be taken to mean that in media cultures the only media outputs are those of the mass media. The point is rather that in media cultures manifestations of a non-mass media culture such as sculpture, painting and buildings depend upon the mass media if they wish to enter the domain of communicative discourse for a particular public. Systems of mass media dynamize cultures; they enlarge publics and alter cultural manifestations through the transformation of their means of production, mediation, reception and processing, in turn increasing both risks and opportunities. The traditional distinction made between experiences conveyed through media and those which are not becomes irrelevant, since the omnipresence of media outputs transforms both the individual and the social construction of reality: 'The culture programme is realized as media culture, and one could almost add: and as nothing else' (Schmidt 1992: 447).

Here it should be noted that in later publications Schmidt has distanced himself from one basic principle of radical constructivism:

21

the necessarily biological foundation of its theory of cognition. Increasingly he considered the 'connection to biology and a theory of cognition' (Schmidt 2003: 24) to be problematic, but without breaking with the underlying biologically oriented functionalism of radical constructivism. In some of his more recent publications, for example, he has sought to reveal the significant roles played by the careers of certain topics in media culture societies (Schmidt 2008: 67; also 2010: 182–8).

Apart from whether we should regard such an approach as *radical* constructivism, or perhaps instead treat it as an approach to the description of 'media culture societies' (Schmidt's latest conceptual coining [2008]) in which systems 'flirt' with each other, it can be said that our understanding of the nature of media culture is definitely advanced by Schmidt's arguments, even if they do also introduce a number of unresolved problems. He makes very clear that media culture is *constitutive of reality*. By this I mean that Schmidt and his radical constructivist associates have quite rightly emphasized that one cannot speak meaningfully of media culture on account of the fact that in these cultures all communication processes are founded upon technical media. It does, however, make sense to talk of media culture if the construction of reality in individual cultures relies for what is culturally specific in this process upon media. To be more specific: it is not characteristic of media cultures that all humans communicate with each other, mediated only by technical media. It is instead more characteristic of media culture that if humans communicate directly with each other, then media constructions of reality are constantly a key reference point of the articulation of meaning. At root it is this point that is made by stating that in media cultures technical media are constitutive of reality.

However, and disregarding here the biological overtones (see the critique by Reichertz 2009: 166), the functionalist assumptions of this approach are hardly capable of grasping the contradictory and complex nature of today's media cultures. Contemporary media cultures are precisely *not* a medially mediated 'programme' governing our construction of reality in a way ultimately aimed at social integration. There are many 'dysfunctional' elements and 'contradictions' in today's media cultures. On top of that, the entire line of argument presumes that this is really all about the culture of national societies, into which persons are to be integrated. In this respect, too, there are shortcomings in the argument. Given the globalized nature of media communication, there is a diversity of media cultures that have no direct relation to any one national society. It is not a matter of 'flirting' with systems (theory) in respect of, and within, 'media culture societies', to freely adapt one of Schmidt's metaphors. Our horizon and our ambitions must be much wider than this – and that is why media culture is not a programme of (national) integration.

Technologized, But Not a Cyberculture

In this section I would like to deal with another widespread understanding of media culture: that present-day media culture is a cyberculture. To some extent it can be said that this draws upon Medium Theory, since it seeks to represent contemporary media culture in terms of one dominant medium. But there is more to cyberculture than this – or to Internet culture, as it is also known. First of all, the very expression implies that cyberculture is quite different to all previously existing forms of culture. Nothing can be compared with media culture in the form of cyberculture because of the reach and extent of its technical development. This should begin to make clear that we are dealing here not with a more or less consistent theoretical framework – of Critical Theory, Medium Theory or radical constructivism. Instead, we are confronted with a multilayered discourse concerning how cyberculture should be treated as the present form of media culture – a discourse which blurs into popular science and culture. Cyberculture is an idea moulded by novels like William Gibson's *Neuromancer* (1986) or Pat Cadigan's cyborg story *Synners* (199), or films like *Blade Runner* (1982) and *The Matrix* (1999). All these novels and films portray the transgression of the border between human technology and nature.

To outline this discourse we need to refer to some anthologies and textbooks. In their critical introduction to 'new' media the British media studies scholars Martin Lister, Kieran Kelly, Jon Dovey, Seth Giddings and Iain Grant have described cyberculture as follows: 'Cyberculture . . . consists in a mass of new technological things, a wide range of imaginative fictions that have, as it were, seeped through the screens so that they may seem the realistic descriptions of our bewildering everyday lives' (2009: 317).

Writing in David Gauntlett's book *Web.Studies*, David Silver (2000) has elaborated three phases of 'cyberculture studies'. The first of these is 'popular cyberculture'. During this phase, material was written by journalists and published in magazines such as *Wired* and *Mondo 2000* that shared a kind of technological euphoria and who were themselves part of the field which was the object of study. As Silver wrote, taking his cue from Steven Jones (1997) and others, this early interest in cyberculture was characterized by a dualism between 'dystopian rants' and 'utopian raves' (Silver 2000: 20). Whereas 'utopian raves' sums up the position of all those who saw in 'cyberspace' the potential for a positive reorganization of human life, 'dystopian rants' represented all those visions of a negative utopia knocking around in the heads of socially isolated nerds.

Next came a phase of *cyberculture studies*. An example of this is Howard Rheingold's (1993, 1995) work on virtual communities. This American popular science writer, who shared much with the culture of Silicon Valley, described in his book *The Virtual Community* (1995) new forms of communal living in cyberspace. Sherry Turkle was no less euphoric in her book *Life on the Screen* (1995), and this from a sociology professor at MIT. In this book she describes the possibilities of articulating online identities, taking advantage of the net's anonymity to develop games of identity that were not possible in direct communication. As such research demonstrated, during this phase there was a concern to elaborate in a scholarly manner the specificities of communication action and social life 'in cyberspace'. To begin with, the work done in this second phase confronted the possibilities of a cyberculture very optimistically, very much as a reaction against the 'dystopian rants' of the first phase.

David Silver sees the third phase as having dominated since the later 1990s. Here we have *critical cyberculture studies* that detach themselves from an exclusive concern with cyberspace. There is a greater emphasis upon relating the forms of interaction, communitization (*Vergemeinschaftung*) and identity found on the Internet to a 'wider life'. The contrast between the state of being online and that of being offline is not treated as of such great importance as keeping the reciprocal relationship between these two states in view. Four years after the appearance of Silver's article, Laura J. Gurak adopted this position, replacing his contribution with her own in the new edition of the book. She accordingly emphasized that 'context is the key' (Gurak 2004: 28) and called for further work to be done with this in mind.

But this did not mean that a degree of utopianism had vanished from work on cyberculture. One example of this is the writing of the above-mentioned British media specialist David Gauntlett, editor of *Web.Studies*. In 2007 he published online an article in which a media studies 1.0 was contrasted with the 'Media Studies 2.0' of his title (Gauntlett 2007). The first of these is characterized by a tendency to fetishize expert opinion, an orientation to powerful, mostly Western, media institutions and their products, an emphasis on critical ability, and a cautious approach to the Internet. The second ('2.0') overcomes this orientation, taking seriously the sheer variety of public creativity, is capable of incorporating diverse relevant cultural factors, while treating digital media and the Internet as equal to all other media. For Gauntlett, this also meant that the methods employed in communication and media studies required rethinking, while also encouraging those approaches that would involve human creativity in research activity.

Such arguments are not without their own contradictions, above all because of the casual use of the metaphor 'Web 2.0' (see, for example, Everitt and Mills 2009). Gauntlett has taken this idea further and elaborated it in his book *Making is Connecting*. Here he is concerned with the 'power of making, and connecting through creating' (Gauntlett 2011: 1), something that existed long before 'Web 2.0' but which here for the first time found its particular expression. Gauntlett especially emphasizes the collaborative aspects of web activity and seeks to develop and theorize everyday human creativity, not least because his approach is to a great extent political (2011: 12).

Gauntlett's arguments are very stimulating, especially when he relates these to the political critique of technology put forward by Ivan Illich (1973), to whom I referred in the Introduction. There is also a welcome emphasis in Gauntlett's work on the potential that the Internet offers for the creative and productive use of technology, something that Illich considered was absent from the use of technologies from the 1950s to the 1970s. However, problems arise once we move beyond talk of the *potentiality* inhering in particular adoptions to talk generally of a 'new media culture'. This is a project embraced by Henry Jenkins (2006a, 2006b), who was then Professor for Comparative Media Studies at MIT and is an internationally recognized investigator of popular culture. Jenkins favours the concept of 'convergence culture' for the new 'media culture'. He argues that the establishment of the Internet has rendered the popular aspects of media culture more diverse, more open to the everyday activities of users than was the case during the era of dominant mass media. For Jenkins, convergence means not simply a technical process of integration of different digital platforms, but a coming together of 'old' and 'new' media in today's media cultures. As he writes, by convergence he means 'the flow of content across multiple media platforms, the co-operation between multiple media industries, and the migratory behaviour of media audiences who will go almost anywhere in search of the kinds of entertainment experiences they want' (2006a: 2). Understood in this way, convergence is a 'cultural shift' (2006a: 2) generally characteristic of contemporary popular cultures: consumers in 'convergence cultures' are much more closely bound into the processes of media production than was hitherto the case. Jenkins also sees convergence as closely related with new forms of participation and collective intelligence: 'convergence encourages participation and collective intelligence' (2006a: 245).

These two examples make quite clear how the utopianism of the early cyberculture years has been absorbed into scholarly research on actual use of the Internet. This should be no cause for surprise. Of help here is the work of Manuel Castells – an urban sociologist and one of the best-known investigators of network society – on what he has called the 'culture of the Internet' (Castells 2001: 36). If we relate Castells' work to our discussion here, it becomes apparent that much of the utopianism of historical and current interest in cyberculture relates to a 'culture of production' (Negus 1997) typical of early Internet adopters. Following on from this, Castells describes 'the culture of the creators of the Internet . . . [as] a set of values and beliefs informing behaviour' (2001: 36). Castells argues that Internet culture is developed from four cultural moments. The first of these is a 'techno-meritocratic culture', anchored in academia and the natural sciences, operating within scholarly traditions such as 'peer review' and free access to knowledge. Second comes 'hacker culture', which lays emphasis on the freedom of technical development or unrestricted communication, whose currently most obvious manifestation is the Open Source movement, or WikiLeaks. Third comes the 'virtual communitarian culture', which is aimed at the realization of alternative lifestyles within and through online communities. Finally there is a specific 'entrepreneurial culture'. Here the entrepreneurial spirit assumes a particular form, since – in their perspective – 'Internet entrepreneurs are creators rather than businessmen, closer to the artists' culture than to the traditional corporate culture' (Castells 2001: 60). To some extent they seek to flee from society, using technology to make a large amount of money and through this 'personal accumulation of wealth' (Castells 2001: 58) free themselves of any constraint. These four moments form a 'four-layer' structure, as Castells (2001: 37) describes the Internet culture: 'The culture of the Internet is a culture made up of a technocratic belief in the progress of humans through technology, enacted by communities of hackers thriving on free and open technological creativity, embedded in virtual networks aimed at reinventing society, and materialized by money-driven entrepreneurs into the workings of new economy' (Castells 2001: 61).

If we consider the utopianism of cyberculture as discussed above from this perspective, it is plain that its arguments represent what

Castells calls the production culture of today's Internet – or what we can simply call Internet culture. What significance the Internet, or digital media technologies, might have for contemporary culture remains another question. If one takes this as the central perspective for the study of media culture it quickly becomes clear that today's media cultures are not simply cybercultures, and that one needs to treat with care the tendency to treat dystopian or utopian conceptions of the Internet as a point of departure for describing media culture. As Castells shows in this regard, the position is much more complex.

Even if this use of cyberculture as a convenient shorthand for (present) media culture has real limitations, there are some things that can be learned from work on cybercultures. This approach first of all makes clear the importance of media technologies in the change of today's media cultures. Secondly, it shows how changes in the forms of communicating indicate changes in the 'objects' with which we communicate. Thirdly, it shows how necessary it is to reflect in a new way on our relationship with 'the objects of media technology'. Here the study of cyberculture above has made clear that the establishment of digital media – first and foremost the media of the Internet – suggests a comprehensive shift in culture. If media culture has not become cyberculture, we still should note that today media cultures are technicized cultures.

3

The Mediatization of Culture

As we have seen in the previous chapter, there are many points to consider if we are to clarify the character of media culture. We can say with some certainty that it is not mass culture, nor is it a dominating or guiding culture, or a cultural programme, or a cyberculture. But we have to bear in mind that media culture is something related to the increasing omnipresence of media communication, that it is moulded by various media in different ways; further, that it is constitutive of reality, and that we need to take account of the increasing reliance of communication on particular technologies. I now want to show that on this basis we should conceive 'media culture' as a shorthand for the mediatization of culture: media cultures are the cultures of mediatization. This will make it possible to deal with the various issues of omnipresence, moulding, constitution of reality and the role of technology without ending up with yet another understanding which is partial in one way or another.

But what does mediatization mean? We can begin clarification of this through a discussion of arguments advanced by John B. Thompson, whose book *The Media and Modernity* discusses the manner in which the development of European modernity is related to the establishment of media. His point of departure is that the classics of the social sciences, social historians and historically informed sociologists have all addressed themselves to the principal features of the transformation of institutions that occurred in the shift from the late Middle Ages into modernity

(Thompson 1995: 45). This line of argument deals first of all with the economic transformation from European feudalism to a system of capitalist production, trade and finance, together with the political transformation of a large number of principalities and kingdoms into national states, and also the military changes in which these national states became the sole bearers of legitimate force. Thompson suggests that previous work has been very contradictory in its treatment of cultural change. His view is that insufficient weight has been given to the role of media communication in this process of transformation. It has always been a question of whether values changed with the emergence of modernity, or to what extent values changed, and if so, which ones. Responses to these questions have been varied. However, cultural change can be examined much more clearly if we shift our attention from values to symbolic forms. This is where 'mediatization' comes in, or, as Thompson calls it, 'mediazation':

> If we focus ... not on values, attitudes, and beliefs, but rather on symbolic forms and their modes of production and circulation in the social world, then we shall see that, with the advent of modern societies in the late medieval and early modern periods, a systematic cultural transformation began to take hold. By virtue of a series of technical innovations associated with printing and, subsequently, with the electrical codification of information, symbolic forms were produced, reproduced, and circulated on a scale that was unprecedented. Patterns of communication and interaction began to change in profound and irreversible ways. These changes, which comprise what can loosely be called the 'mediazation of culture', had a clear institutional basis: namely, the development of media organizations, which first appeared in the second half of the fifteenth century and have expanded their activities ever since. (Thompson 1995: 46)

For Thompson, mediatization is not then a linear process, but something which occurs in a number of distinct waves. He refers to an 'extended mediazation' in respect of the 1990s (Thompson 1995: 110). By this he means the increasingly self-referential nature of mass communications, the way in which newspapers and TV treat items carried in other media – for example, an interview given by a politician the day before – as objects for their own reportage. Generally, Thompson identifies a 'mediazation of tradition' (1995: 180), by which he means the transformation of lived tradition into symbolic content. This came about because it became possible to communicate through media traditions to locations other than those in which they originated.

Although Thompson's book appeared some years ago, its arguments are very close to what I will call in the following the mediatization of culture. It will become clear that mediatization did not just originate with the establishment of digital media but is a longer-term process. It will also become clear that this is a matter not merely of the transformation of media, but also of the transformation of symbolic forms, and so of communication bound up with the media. And it will become evident that this process of mediatization can develop in distinct phases, that there are particular caesuras and upheavals. At root – and this seems to me to be the principal issue – the above quote from Thompson shows that mediatization is a concept that seeks to capture the shifting interrelationship between change, on the one hand, and socio-cultural media-communicative change, on the other.

This maps out the line of argument to be pursued in the following chapters. I want to begin by making a more precise distinction between the concept of mediatization and that of mediation. This then leads to examination of the idea that study of mediatization should in particular distance itself from questions of media logic(s). In criticizing this stance I arrive at a conception of mediatization as a metaprocess, or as a panorama, concluding with a more detailed investigation of the moulding forces of the media as part of this metaprocess. And this brings us back to the question of what an appropriate theorization of technology might look like.

Mediatization and Mediation

There is a particularly anglophone controversy about the manner in which 'mediatization' might be distinguished from 'mediation' – something that would in German be expressed as *Mediatisierung* and *Vermittlung*, respectively. Nick Couldry (2008) and Sonia Livingstone (2009: 6f.) have made clear the fuzziness of the distinction. They agree on a preference for the concept of mediation over that of mediatization. However, it should however be noted that, more recently, Couldry (2012: 134–7) has begun to emphasize the utility of the concept of mediatization. I will come back to this. But firstly I want to deal with the concept of mediation, if only in a relatively cursory and far from complete manner. This concept has to be demarcated from that of mediatization, as was pointed out long ago by the American sociologist Ernest Manheim, a Hungarian émigré who in 1933 completed in Germany a dissertation on 'The Bearers (*Träger*) of Public Opinion'. In this dissertation he dealt with the mediatization of direct human relationships, something which he considered of greater significance than simple mediation (cf. Averbeck-Lietz 2011).

It can be said quite generally that the importance attached to the concept of mediation in the study of media and communication is not confined to the English-speaking world. In Germany there are signs that the study of media and communications is likewise taking an interest in questions of mediation. In this connection we can refer to an almost forgotten classical figure in journalism studies, Otto Groth. He has remained of interest not least because of the way that, from the 1920s, he developed a perspective on newspapers and journalism which placed them in a cultural framework (see Langenbucher 1998; Wagner 1998; Hepp 2004: 27–44), among other reasons because of the instrumentalization of journalism studies by the National Socialist regime. This was examined by Groth in his *History of German Journalism Studies* (1948), leading to the publication in the 1960s of his six-volume book *The Unrecognized Cultural Power*.

Central to this work for Groth is the category of *mediation* (*Vermittlung*): his treatment of journalism studies does not assume that journalists are 'transmitters' who 'convey' news to 'receivers', but begins directly with the 'cultural work' of the newspaper itself. According to Groth, the significance of a newspaper or a periodical lies in the 'mediation of social communication', a conception that was explicitly directed against a series of 'transmission models'

(Grossberg et al. 1998: 16) that were prevalent in the early years of German-language journalism studies. Hence Groth criticized the idea that a newspaper was a means of 'journalistic expression', as for instance Hans Traub had argued in a 1933 study of journalists as producers. The principal counterargument that Groth advances is that the expression of particular contents is only a 'precondition' (Groth 1960: 544) of the mediating function of a newspaper. He wishes to direct attention instead to the 'reciprocity' or the 'interrelation' existing between the creators of media and their recipients. The basic precondition of any need for mediation is, on the one hand,

> *an intervening space or a difference, a distance or a tension*, whether intellectual or physical, between partners – a gap whose bridging, removal or dissolution is desired; and on the other the capacity of relating particular points through such mediation, despite all separation and difference, thereby bringing about *connection and concord*.
> (Groth 1960: 564, original emphases)

For Groth, this 'intervening space' or 'distance' indicates the existence of communication partners in a society, partners who are mediated by a medium. This existing 'distance' does, however, have further cultural implications, beyond the limited model of the process of communication. For Groth, 'the number of intervening spaces and tensions between people has become more numerous across a world dominated by the increasingly individualized culture of high capitalism' (1960: 615). On the one hand there are clearly processes of atomization and individualization. But on the other hand in 'high capitalism' there is also the dynamic of massification and uniformity. Ultimately there is a cultural necessity for mediation exactly *because* of the way that different partners to communication are embedded in different (local) contexts.

Even in these decades-old ideas the basic elements of a sound understanding of mediation are apparent: this conception involves a perspective upon media communication that transcends the idea of 'transmission' expressed in Lasswell's formulation 'who says what in which channel to whom with what effect?' (1961:

117). At stake is the theorization of a highly complex communicative relationship between different actors standing one with another in direct communication, which relationship then alters when media become part of this mediation process. And so it is not simply a matter of satisfactorily distinguishing the different levels of, respectively, 'mediation' and 'mediatization'. Of equal if not greater importance is what the investigation of mediatization can learn from the study and theorization of processes of mediation.

The point of reference for international discussion has been less the contribution made by German theoreticians than that of Latin Americans, foremost among them Jesús Martín-Barbero. Martín-Barbero was born in Spain but has spent much of his career teaching in Mexico and Columbia. In his book *Communication, Culture, and Hegemony*, originally published in 1987, he called for a reorientation of the analysis of communications and media 'from media to mediations' (Martín-Barbero 1993: 187). He is concerned first of all to conceive (media) communication as a meeting point of quite diverse forces of conflict and integration, analysing them in these terms. It is important here to identify the socially situated nature of media communication: 'We had to lose sight of the "proper object" in order to find the way to the movement of the social in communication, to communication in process' (Martín-Barbero 1993: 203). Behind this is an experience that Martín-Barbero shares with other Latin American social and cultural scientists: that the existing approaches to the description of (mass) media as instances of ideology and the transfer of information are inadequate for understanding the increasingly 'hybrid cultures' (García Canclini 1995) of Latin America in all their globalized conflict and commercialization. It is for this reason that he develops an approach which proposes 'to start with the mediations where the social materialization and the cultural expression of television are delimited and configured' (Martín-Barbero 1993: 215). For him this is the social life of the family, social temporality and cultural competence. With respect to the family, it is not simply a matter of treating it as a context for the appropriation of media – especially that of television. It is equally the object of media and its narratives. TV formats therefore involve 'mediators' (1993: 216) between the everyday world and a fictional family world. It is similar for social temporality, in which series and TV genres are 'mediators between the time of capital and the time of daily experience' (1993: 219). So far as cultural competence is concerned, it is quite evident that today television is a central instance of mediation.

Hence, following Martín-Barbero's lead, we can describe media communication, more exactly TV, as a process of mediation of the 'logics of production and use' (1993: 221). It is not a simple matter of a capitalist logic of production, for example, having an impact upon the logics of use and so upon people's everyday lives. The situation is much more complex, involving the mediation of different logics, a plurality of logics. In respect of TV, the different genres appear as the central instance of mediation. As Martín-Barbero expresses it:

> The genres are the mediation between the logic of the productive system and the logics of use. . . . The study of genres as strategies of interaction or as ways in which senders and receivers organize and make their communicative abilities recognizable is impossible without reconceptualizing the meaning of communication. . . . If seen as moments of *renegotiation*, genres cannot be approached in terms of semantics or syntax. They require the construction of a communicative pragmatics that can capture the operation of their recognition by a cultural community. (1993: 223–4, emphasis in original)

This quote crystallizes the core of Martín-Barbero's approach to media communication as a process of mediation: 'He seeks to grasp interaction as a totality before using this to develop an analysis of the power of communication. This approach is deliberately aimed against any treatment of media communication primarily in terms of production. Such an approach would, Martín-Barbero argues, be too simplistic, since the impact of a 'logic of the productive system' (1993: 223) would be suited to other spheres of the social, and not the 'moments of renegotiation' that play a genuinely constitutive role in communication.

If we adopt this broad understanding of media communication

as mediation, it is possible to see that Stuart Hall's 'encoding–decoding' model (1980) or later approaches that deal with media communication as a 'circuit of culture' do in fact represent mediational conceptions (see, for example, Johnson 1986; du Gay et al. 1997). Beyond the basic approaches that Grossberg, Wartella and Whitney have characterized as a 'cultural model' (Grossberg et al. 1998: 18), it was Roger Silverstone especially who examined in detail mediation as a basic key concept for the sciences of communication and media.

Silverstone takes an approach similar to that of Martín-Barbero without, however, referring to the latter's work. His book *Why Study the Media?* systematically treated media communication as a 'process of mediation' (1999: 13) that does not stop with the reception of a media product: 'Mediation involves the movement of meaning from one text to another, from one discourse to another, from one event to another' (1999: 13). But this process of mediation is more than the kind of two-step flow envisaged by classical media and communication scholars such as Elihu Katz and Paul Lazarsfeld (1955). This mediation is not simply a matter of gathering views about media content from opinion leaders. Silverstone treats mediation in much the same manner as Martín-Barbero, as a much more extended process in which we 'engage continuously and infinitely with media meanings' (Silverstone 1999: 17). He argues that media research cannot only be about a 'mechanics of mediation' embedded in media texts and technologies (1999: 29). From his point of view this is the first step, but not enough in itself. Beyond that there has to be 'an understanding of the proper location of the textual claim, historically, sociologically, anthropologically' (1999: 37) in everyday life. The accent that Silverstone brings to this is based upon his argument that mediation is in principle open-ended, involving an endless process: '[M]ediation is endless, the product of textual unravelling in the words, deeds, and experience of everyday life, as much as by the continuities of broadcasting and narrowcasting. ... Mediation is in this sense less determined, more open, more singular, more shared, more vulnerable, perhaps, to abuse' (1999: 15).

This exemplary theorization of 'mediation' makes clear what

is at stake here: it is about the development of a perspective upon media communication which is capable of reflecting its actual integration with social and cultural contexts or processes. In so doing we break with a linear perspective that begins with media production, derives particular characteristics of media contents from this, then moves to the reception and effect of these contents. The concept of mediation involves a more complex approach to reciprocal interrelationships saturated with power and which become concrete in the process of media communication. This perspective pulls Latin American research on media and culture together with European cultural studies (Martín-Barbero 2006). In addition to this we have a basic conception generally suited for dealing with the study of media and culture from a cultural-analytic orientation. The Swedish researcher Johan Fornäs has consequently talked of '*mediation* as a key concept in cultural studies' (2000: 48).

There is some weight to these arguments, and in no respect do I wish to dispute the adoption of mediation as a key concept for the study of communication and media, as well as for cultural studies. The positions outlined above are robust and there is a great deal to be said for treating media communication in general as a process of mediation, and not conceive it as the simple transfer of information, as was typical of the early days of media research. Nor is there much to add to Silverstone's contention that this mediating process is open-ended in principle.

Because of the underlying and foundational character of the concept of mediation it does not seem to me very productive to treat 'mediation' and 'mediatization' as *opposing exclusive conceptions*. This is not because one could learn nothing from such a contrast. Nick Couldry (2008) has, for example, been able to show that some particular variations of the conception of mediatization tend to be linear, a tendency absent from the approaches taken by Martín-Barbero and Silverstone.

What is, however, problematic in drawing such a contrast is the implication that both conceptions *are on the same level*: each would seek to capture the same phenomena, and their interrelation has therefore to be discussed. It is for this reason that they need to be distinguished. If we go back to the quotation from Thompson with which we started this chapter, it is clear that the conception of mediatization is much more specific than that of mediation. While mediation is suited to describing the general characteristics of any process of media communication, mediatization describes and theorizes something rather different, something that is *based on* the mediation of media communication: *mediatization seeks to capture the nature of the interrelationship between historical changes in media communication and other transformational processes*. Hence mediatization *presumes* mediation through media communication. Consideration of processes of mediatization is conducted at the level of ongoing processes of transformation which, in each particular instance, are associated with a variety of specific mediations through media communication. Hence it is not a question of whether we need to use 'mediatization' *or* 'mediation' in our approach to contemporary media cultures. Instead, we need both of them, since they relate to different things.

Media Logic(s)

If we examine *how* mediatization has been treated and operationalized by existing research on mediatization, we repeatedly encounter a conception that Martín-Barbero also mentions, that of a 'logic'. But the fact that mediatization research refers to this in the singular suggests an emphasis different from that of Martín-Barbero: it is a matter not of logics associated with the reciprocities of production and use, but of a 'media logic' which, with the advance of mediatization, increasingly exercises influence over spheres that are 'beyond the media'. As we shall see, underlying this there is a specific concept of media: media as institutions of mass communication – above all, television.

The concept of a media logic is always linked back to the book of the same name published in 1979 by two American researchers, David L. Altheide and Robert P. Snow. Their point of departure was the condition of American mass communications research at the time, a practice whose focus was on media contents and their public influence. Altheide and Snow employed arguments drawn from symbolic interactionism, ethnomethodology and phenomenology to suggest that existing practice was poorly framed and directed, since 'the role of media in our lives' (Altheide and Snow 1979: 7) was reduced to one among many variables affecting social processes. To understand the 'role of media' they argued that it was necessary to ask *how* the media as a 'form of communication' (1979: 9) transform our perception and our interpretation of the social. The conception of media logic is intended to capture this. Altheide and Snow describe this as follows:

> In general terms, *media logic* consists of a form of communication; the process through which media present and transmit information. Elements of this form include the various media and the formats used by these media. Format consists, in part, of how material is organized, the style in which it is presented, the focus or emphasis on particular characteristics of behaviour, and the grammar of media communication. Format becomes a framework or a perspective that is used to present as well as interpret phenomena. . . . Thus, the logic of media formats has become so taken for granted by both communicator and receiver that it has been overlooked as an important factor in understanding media. (1979: 10, emphasis in original)

Altheide and Snow establish, through a critical re-evaluation of classical sociological writings by Georg Simmel and Erving Goffman, that a media logic inheres not in media contents, but in the form of media communication. The latter should be understood as a 'processual framework *through which* social action occurs' (1979: 15, emphasis in original) – in this case, the social action of communication. This media logic as form is especially evident in the formats of mass communications, which Altheide and Snow treat as a connecting element in the entire process of the mediation of media communication – here there is a clear affinity with the work of Martín-Barbero. Both authors retained this view of media logic in their later publications when dealing with the analysis of the forms and formats of mediation (see, for example, Altheide and Snow 1988; Altheide 2004).

Borrowing from James Monaco (1978) and developing these

ideas, Altheide and Snow were already describing late 1970s American culture as a media culture. They meant by this that a media logic was beginning to exert an influence upon institutions which were not media institutions, strictly speaking. Their examples drew upon religion, politics and sport. These institutions – or, as we would perhaps say today, social fields – are marked for Altheide and Snow by the way in which their realities are increasingly articulated according to a media logic. As they themselves write, '[W]hen a media logic is employed to present and interpret institutional phenomena, the form and content of those institutes are altered . . . every major institution has become part of media culture' (Altheide and Snow 1979: 11)

It is this basic understanding of mediatization as the *permeation* of a media logic into other institutions, social fields or social systems – a media logic which is initially linked to institutions of mass communication – which forms the core of many analyses done in this area (cf. Mazzoleni 2008b; Meyen 2009; Schrott 2009; Strömbäck and Esser 2009). Possibly the most prominent among these are the works of Winfried Schulz and Stig Hjarvard, which is why I will deal with these writers in greater detail below.

Building in part on ideas that he had developed with Gianpietro Mazzoleni (1999), Schulz (2004) set about 'reconstructing mediatization as an analytic concept'. He treats the permeation of a media logic as only *one* moment of mediatization, distinguishing four aspects of mediatization: extension, substitution, amalgamation and accommodation.

Extension takes up the idea already proposed by Marshall McLuhan (McLuhan and Lewis 1994) within the framework of Medium Theory, discussed above, that the media are 'extensions of man': that is, extensions of the possibilities of communicative action related to place, time and means of expression. Mediatization here means that the possibilities of human communicative action have increased with the passage of time. *Substitution* describes the fact that media have, wholly or in part, replaced social activities and social institutions. Schulz points to video and computer games which replace forms of face-to-face play. This is therefore a matter of how forms mediated by the media can displace non-media-mediated forms, this being a further moment of mediatization. *Amalgamation* describes the way in which action related to the media and action not so related become increasingly blurred into one another. There are everyday examples of this that we can imagine, such as the combination of an activity unrelated to the media (driving a car) with one related to the media (listening to the radio); or using a mobile to arrange appointments while engaged on manual tasks at work. In this sense mediatization is a progressive process of amalgamation between media-related and non-media-related activities. Finally we come to *accommodation*, and Schulz here uses the concept of media logic. He suggests that there is a tendency in different areas of society (politics, sport, and so forth) to become orientated to a 'media logic', describing this primarily as a staging process effected by the use of television (Schulz 2004: 89). For Schulz, therefore, mediatization is *also* the diffusion of a media logic, but not exclusively so.

It is worth noting that Schulz discusses the question of the role played by the establishment of digital media in the advance of mediatization. Are there moments that are more regressive than progressive for mediatization? For Schulz, this question seems an obvious one, since he treats mediatization as a product 'of the television era' (2004: 94). He rejects an equivocal conclusion in which an 'optimistic answer' – digital media mean the end of the mediatization of mass communications – is balanced by a 'sceptical answer' – we are confronted with new and sometimes problematic modes of mediatization, arguing instead for a 'moderate answer': new digital media do not simply displace or replace previously existing mass media, which is why 'the mediatization effects of the latter endure in the new media environment' (2004: 98). Consequently he considers that his concept of mediatization is suited to the investigation of further media change.

The Danish media and communication researcher Stig Hjarvard has a rather different approach, shaping his concept of mediatization around that of media logic. His point of departure is identical to what we have seen in Altheide and Snow, even when he relates his concept of mediatization more strongly to Scandinavian research (especially Asp 1990). Hjarvard likewise claims that if we want to capture the influence of media upon culture and society it is no longer sufficient to ask after the effects of media contents. We need instead a broader perspective that takes account of the way in which culture and society are today saturated with media. This is where he introduces his conception of mediatization, describing his approach as an 'institutional perspective' (Hjarvard 2008: 110). He makes two points, in so doing distinguishing himself from Schulz. First of all, he is concerned with the analysis of the relationships between media as institutions and other social institutions. Secondly, and following on from this, he seeks to use the concept of mediatization to refer only to a *particular form* of the institutionalization of the media: 'autonomous' social institutionalization, which he argues is the precondition for media institutions *as such* exerting an influence over other social institutions. For Europe since the 1980s he considers this condition to be given, as media (he includes alongside institutions of mass communication both mobile and Internet communication) became increasingly commercialized quite independently of 'public steering' (Hjarvard 2008: 120). Only from this point can one speak meaningfully of mediatization, according to Hjarvard:

> By the mediatization of society, we understand the process whereby society to an increasing degree is submitted to, or becomes dependent on, the media and their logic. This process is characterized by a duality in that the media have become *integrated* into the operations of other social institutions, while they have also acquired the status of social institutions *in their own right*. As a consequence, social interaction – within the respective institutions, between institutions, and in society at large – take [*sic*] place via the media. The term 'media logic' refers to the institutional and technological modus operandi of the media, including the ways in which media distribute material and symbolic resources and operate with the help of informal rules. (2008: 113, emphasis in original)

This is a very particular development of the conception of media logic, treating it in terms of an *institutional* media logic (cf. Hjarvard 2009: 160). As independent institutions that increasingly pervade our contemporary lives, media have developed their own logic. Mediatization accordingly means increasing independence of, and subordination to, this logic.

Hjarvard distinguishes two modes of mediatization: 'strong', direct mediatization and 'weak', indirect mediatization (2004: 48f.; 2008: 114). *Direct mediatization* describes those moments in which action not hitherto mediated by media is turned into a form mediated by media: that is, action with and by means of a medium. One example Hjarvard notes is the game of chess, which has become a computer or online game. *Indirect mediatization* occurs when the form, content or organization of an action becomes increasingly influenced by symbols or mechanisms specific to the media. An example of this would be the mediatization of politics, a reference often made in this institutional perspective (Kepplinger 2002; Vowe 2006; Strömbäck 2008; Mazzoleni 2008a). Somewhat remarkably, Hjarvard claims that direct and indirect forms of mediatization continually appear together, which, apart from anything else, makes it hard to tell the one from the other (2008: 115). One can think of the game of poker, which is 'directly' mediatized in the form of TV or online poker, but is at the same time 'indirectly' mediatized in that poker continues to be played at home and in pubs, but is marked in different ways by its staging in the media (Hitzler and Möll 2012). Here there is a degree of convergence of Hjarvard's ideas with those of Schulz. Hence we could say that 'direct mediatization' points to 'substitution', while 'indirect mediatization' points to 'accommodation', and the lack of a clearcut distinction between these two further suggests Schulz's conception of 'amalgamation'. The fact that Hjarvard does not identify the moment of 'extension' is to do with his institutional conception of mediatization: according to him, 'extension' is a general moment of 'mediation' of media communication and does not relate specifically to the process of mediatization, which only developed in a true sense in Europe from the 1980s onwards.

But comprehensive criticisms have also been made of these developments of mediatization as (institutionalized) media logic. Probably the strongest of these come from Nick Couldry and Knut Lundby, although they do differ quite markedly in the vehemence of their critique.

Couldry comes at this from his adherence to belief in the open-ended nature of processes of mediation; and his critique of the idea that mediatization represents the diffusion of a media logic has two main points. First, the influence of media is far too heterogeneous to be reduced to 'a single "media logic", as if they all operated in one direction, at the same speed, through a parallel mechanism and according to the same calculus of probability' (Couldry 2008: 378; cf. also Couldry 2012: 135–1). Couldry believes that the expression 'media logic' – reinforced by its use in the singular – implies a unity of influence on the part of the media that is rarely, if at all, to be found. This is even more true with the subsequent differentiation of the media, with the development of the Internet, for example. Following on from Couldry, we might note that politics is at present confronted with very different and sometimes contradictory moments of media influence: not only the particular staging strategies of visual communication, but also the wholesale questioning of established secrecy politics through, for instance, WikiLeaks. Secondly, Couldry argues that 'media logic' suggests that there is a 'linear nature' (2008: 377) in the process of change. He takes as his example Schulz's idea of substitution, which, as we have seen, is echoed by Hjarvard's conception of indirect mediatization. Mediatization conceived as the permeation of a media logic in various social institutions is at least tendentially a linear narrative. One is often reminded of 1970s modernization theory, according to which, for example, modern role models in the media gradually contribute to modernization by questioning the way in which people lead their lives (Lerner 1977; for criticism see Hepp 2006). The dialectic of the reciprocities in the change of media communication, on the one hand, and ongoing social and cultural change, on the other, seems to be a great deal more complex than such narratives allow.

The Norwegian media and communication researcher Knut Lundby does not express himself so forcefully, but is nonetheless critical of the idea of mediatization as the autonomous diffusion of a media logic. He defends the arguments of Hjarvard and suggests that these are far less linear than they might at first appear (Lundby 2009: 106). However, he does argue that the use of the expression 'media logic' is misleading if this is treated as a *unitary* logic 'behind' the media and neglects the way in which the constraints upon the change of media themselves alter over time (2009: 104f.). Presenting a moderate critique, he argues that the origins of the conception of media logic should be taken seriously: an origin which lies in the work of Georg Simmel, and the way in which this formed the point of departure for the work of Altheide and Snow. In Simmel the concept of form relates to the structuring of social interaction according to characteristic patterns. If we take this up, then investigation of mediatization has to be more open to, and concerned about, the question of the influence of forms of media communication. Lundby puts it like this:

> I conclude that it is not viable to speak of an overall media logic: it is necessary to specify how various media capabilities are applied in various patterns of social interactions. It is not that a media logic does not involve social interaction, which, not least, Stig Hjarvard's work makes clear. My argument is rather that a focus on a general media logic hides these patterns of interaction. . . . Hence, one has to study how transformations and changes in the mediatization processes take place in communication. Mediatization research should put emphasis upon how social and communicative forms are developed when media are taken into use in social interaction. (2009: 117)

One cannot but agree with this call for more open-ended research into mediatization, yet the idea of a media logic brings with it many other problems. For one thing, this model presumes a model of a functionally differentiated society in which 'the media' are a specifically institutionalized social system charged with the function of public communication and, in this way, facilitating a social or cultural discourse of self-understanding. Only with this assumption does it make sense for other institutions to bend to the 'logics' of the media. While of course media institutions *also* play a role in the overall social communication of the national state, they are a great deal more than functional systems. And if media communication penetrates various social spheres, it is hardly appropriate to reduce them all to one primary functional system. Society and culture, like media communication, are too diverse to equate mediatization, however understood, with the diffusion of a media logic.

One should here recall Berger and Luckmann's words of warning. In discussing the social construction of institutions, they noted that 'great care is required in any statements one makes about the "logic" of institutions' (1967: 82). And as they go on: 'The logic does not reside in the institutions and their external functionalities, but in the way these are treated in reflection about them. Put differently, reflexive consciousness superimposes the quality of logic on the institutional order' (1967: 82).

From a certain point onwards we are also here dealing with normative questions. If we ascribe a 'logic' to the institutions of the media which in some way works 'by itself', then we forget that it is we human beings who act communicatively with media, and also take responsibility for these actions. And so in the functionalities of media logic we no longer see the acting subjects, the meaningfulness of their action, as well as all the other problems of power in communication.

Mediatization as a Metaprocess and as Panorama

As I have shown in the previous section, it is not enough to treat mediatization as the increasing permeation of a media logic. But if one shares the argument so far, there is one question that arises almost of necessity: what, then, is mediatization? As I will show, the concept of mediatization does not involve a finished theory of media transformation, but is much more open, opening a particular panorama, a particular all-encompassing vision of the treatment of the reciprocal relationship between media-communicative change and socio-cultural change. This becomes all the more clear once we turn to an understanding of mediatization distinct from that dealt with so far. We can find this in the work of Friedrich Krotz, whose book *The Mediatization of Communicative Action* (2001) deals with the concept of mediatization as a metaprocess.

Krotz (2007: 27; 2008a; 2008b; 2009) uses the concept of

'metaprocess' as a basic conception describing a particular kind of theory. According to him, metaprocesses are conceptual constructions with the aid of which we deal with generalized processes of change. Given that these take place over a lengthy period, these processes are not just measurable in the sense that one investigates a certain phenomenon at an initial point in time along defined variables and again at a second point in time, then compares the results and characterizes the differences as change. For one thing this is not practically possible, since the processes with which we are concerned go too far back for such a comparative approach to be of any use. But this approach is also inadequate conceptually, since the various metaprocesses proceed at different levels, for they are multidimensional. Krotz describes metaprocesses of social and cultural change as follows:

> With the concept of metaprocess we wish to make clear that we are dealing with long-lasting broadly based cultural changes, to some extent with process of processes that have a long-term influence upon the social and cultural development of humanity. More precisely, we are dealing with a *conceptual construct*, with the aid of which science and scholarship as well as people comprehend particular changes in their everyday lives, their causes, forms of expression and effects, in this rendering the world manageable. (Krotz 2007: 27, emphasis in original)

From this point of view, we are aware of the different metaprocesses of change: the metaprocess of individualization as the increasing 'release' of the individual from 'status and class' (Beck 1987) and the associated insecurities, politics of choice and new forms of communitization, as well as sub-processes like eventization (Hitzler and Honer 1994; Beck and Beck-Gernsheim 2001; Hitzler 2010); the metaprocess of globalization as an ongoing world-wide increase of connectivity and the associated processes of embedding and dis-embedding (Giddens 1990; Tomlinson 1999; Hepp 2004); the metaprocess of commercialization with the development of various consumer cultures (Featherstone 1991; Urry 1995; Bauman 2007); and, of course, the metaprocess of mediatization.

This understanding of metaprocess suggests a particular concept of theory, distinguishing theories according to their empirical referent (see on the following Krotz et al. 2008b: 12). In relating contextual statements to empirical phenomena – which, paradoxically, themselves only become objects of investigation once a particular theoretical standpoint is adopted – we can distinguish three kinds of theory. These are theories that are either, firstly, mathematically formulable, secondly, substantive theories or, thirdly, metatheories (Table 3.1).

The first type of empirically based theory puts forward a kind of conjecture which is treated as valid until it is refuted through the formation of alternative hypotheses which then find support in quantitative evidence, such as standardized surveys, content analysis, and the like. This is a procedure outlined by Karl Popper in his *The Logic of Scientific Discovery* (1959), which introduced the falsification principle to which theory formation in quantitative research is orientated: the sheer variety of everyday life makes it impossible to apply ratified theoretical principles to all possible cases. Our research should therefore focus on seeking to refute, or

Table 3.1   Types of empirically founded theories

Type 1: Mathematical theories	Type 2: Substantive theories	Type 3: Metatheories
Theories are propositions that describe a delimited domain of mathematically formulable (functional) relationships	Theories are propositions that typify a delimited domain of phenomena in terms of structure and process	Theories are narratives that go beyond particular domains of phenomena and which tend to general explanation
Quantitative procedures as the methodological approach	Qualitative procedures as the methodological approach	Explanation and structuration with relevant empirical foundation as the methodological approach

Source: Based on Krotz (2005: 70); Krotz et al. (2008b: 12).

falsify, plausible theories. This in itself increases our knowledge, for it becomes possible, step by step, to exclude particular theories. Theories of the second type are based on qualitative research and are directed to particular 'fields' that are studied with the aim of developing theory. The common procedure is to develop theory-laden categorical systems through the comparative analysis of relevant material. Metaprocesses such as individualization, globalization, commercialization and mediatization constitute the third type of theory. These are general theoretical constructs resting in part upon empirical evidence, but which are not empirically verifiable in their entirety. Their function is rather to provide a structure to which concrete research can be directed and then ordered. In this respect, the first two types of theory represent 'building blocks' for the third.

We should note that Krotz's definition of a metaprocess as a 'conceptual construct' relates this both to 'science' *and* to 'people . . . in their everyday lives' (Krotz 2007: 27). In our everyday life we also treat change in terms of general narratives of transformation in which individual experience and observation combine. And so in this sense globalization is not simply an academic concept, but also a concept drawn from everyday life used to make sense of long-term changes occurring in different places. From this point of view the concept of metaprocess has affinities to the idea of a panorama that Bruno Latour has developed in his book *Reassembling the Social* (2007).

Latour seeks to use Actor-Network Theory to develop a form of sociology that takes account of the materiality of things, at the same time moving away from the idea of society as something given. He wants to take seriously the 'old questions' of sociology and investigate how, in its different associations, society is possible, how it articulates itself. On this basis he refuses to treat 'society' as a given unity at the macro level, instead articulating this apparent macrostructure through empirically ascertainable chains of connection. But he also establishes that, whether in everyday life or in the sciences, we find 'clamps' (Latour 2007: 187) or 'narratives' (2007: 189), which in relation to a certain area of phenomena 'solve the question of staging the totality'

(2007: 188). To characterize these 'narratives', Latour introduces the concept of panorama. Panoramas 'design a picture which has no gap in it, giving the spectator the powerful impression of being fully immersed in the real world' (2007: 188). This occurs through the panorama representing a section of this real world as a totality. Technological examples of this are control rooms in power stations, or as used by the fire service and the police, in which monitors, presentations, cards, and so forth, create the semblance of a reality. But the metanarratives of change can also be conceived as a (linguistic) panorama.

In this sense it can be said that metaprocesses are panoramas of comprehensive processes of change. On account of this they are important both in everyday life and in academic discourse, since they give us a general impression of the way in which we should 'look at' our experience of the world and our empirical research. But one has to be careful once one starts to reduce 'the world' with which one is confronted to these panoramas. This applies to all the panoramas of scientific metatheory: 'Durkheim's "sui generis society", Luhmann's "autopoetic systems", Bourdieu's "symbolic economy of fields", Beck's "reflexive modernity" are excellent narratives if they prepare us, once the screening has ended, to take up the political tasks of composition; they are misleading if taken as a description of what is the common world' (Latour, 2007: 189).

Latour's use of language is certainly very metaphorical, something that is generally true of his theorization. But his concept of panorama places emphasis upon a point that is also important for Krotz's treatment of the metaprocess of mediatization: it makes no sense to treat metaprocesses in general, or the metaprocess of mediatization in particular, as 'purely macro phenomena' because they relate to culture and society as a whole – the action of individual people as well as general processes of communitization and the social formation. This is also why it is misleading to seek a formal and ahistorical definition of mediatization. The concept of mediatization opens up a particular panorama of the world. However, what mediatization identifies varies according to the given particularities of this metaprocess itself. Krotz puts it like this:

A differentiated and formalized definition of mediatization can and should not be presented here, because mediatization *qua* definition in a given form is always *specific to a particular time and culture,* so that any definition has to be based upon historical investigation. *Mediatization as a process cannot be decontextualized, not on the historical, social and cultural planes. There are quite possibly also specific processes of mediatization that only apply to individual population groups* . . . . (Krotz 2007: 39, emphasis in original)

Does that mean that we have to leave the definition of mediatization entirely open? Certainly not, otherwise it would make no sense to talk of a *specific* panorama. The work of Norbert Elias can be drawn upon here.

Elias used extensive historical sources to trace a very general change that he dubbed 'the civilizing process', as in the title of his best-known book. This process is not for Elias simply one of increasing (technical) progress. Instead, he studies development as the control of human emotion – feelings of shame, discomfort, for example. He was interested in 'specific changes in the structure of human relations and the corresponding changes in the structure of the psychic habitus' (Elias 2000: 367). Later Elias integrated the question of communication into analysis of these processes, using the framework of his 'symbol theory', which was the title of his last book (1991).

We can learn a very great deal from Elias about the nature of processes of social and cultural change. He draws our attention to the fact that such change – or development, as he calls it – can in no sense be conceived as evolutionary. The reason for this is that 'the instrument of transmission and change' (1991: 23) is different in biological evolution to that in socio-cultural development. In the first case it is 'an organic structure called the "gene"', which in the process of evolution alters, and whose material nature is well defined and stable. In the second case, 'the chief instruments of transmission and change are symbols in the wide sense of the word including not only knowledge but, for example, also standards of conduct and sentiment' (1991: 23). These symbols are, unlike genes, very much more changeable; in particular, they are independent of any change in the evolution of the developed capacity of human speech, and in a comparatively short period. Symbols are specific to individual human groups, to individual cultures and to individual societies. Correspondingly, no unitary tendency of cultural and social change can be detected in the development processes as there are particular retrogressive movements, upheavals or other kind of sudden change: '[I]n contract to evolutionary order, the developmental order is in a qualified manner reversible' (1991: 33). A linear view of cultural and social change therefore seems inadequate, which is why we cannot regard mediatization simply as the 'evolution of communication' (Merten 1994; see also Stöber 2003a, 2003b).

Gebhard Rusch has also emphasized that evolutionary ideas of progress inhere in the conception of media change. He contends that 'the concept of evolution in cultural research is strongly marked by the idea of cultural progress, by the idea of the development of human capacities and knowledge, that social structures and technology are on the same, intertwined, track towards growing self-knowledge, improved and expanded competences forming social reality and dominating nature' (Rusch 2008: 62). We do not have to go as far here as Bruno Latour's (1993) exaggerated thesis that we have never been modern; we can develop a more careful analysis along the lines suggested by Norbert Elias, emphasizing the fundamental difference between biological evolution and socio-cultural change. An 'evolutionary perspective on media transformation' should present no obstacle to an understanding of the complexity and contradictory nature of the changes with which we are actually confronted. It suggests a functionality of progress. But much more care is here needed in using the concept of mediatization.

We can shed rather more light on this idea if we limit this discussion of mediatization as metaprocess and panorama to Europe since early modern times. Here it is helpful to introduce a heuristic distinction between the quantitative and the qualitative aspects of mediatization.

Firstly, the *quantitative aspects of mediatization* are associated with the word 'more'. It is perfectly evident that the sheer number of communications media available to us has increased, if not in a strictly linear way. The same goes for the different ways in which these media are appropriated. This itself breaks up any idea of linearity, for the ways of dealing with media have become ever more varied and numerous, and with this the possibilities and impossibilities of their 'influence'. The ongoing dispersion of technically mediated communication can, quantitatively, be distinguished in terms of (a) time, (b) space and (c) the social (Krotz 2007: 37–41). We can summarize the key elements of the last few years in Europe as follows:

- *Over time*, an increasing number of technologically mediated forms of communication have become permanently available. For example, television no longer closes down for the night, but has become an endless 'flow' (Williams 2003) of technically mediated communication. Or alternatively, the Internet makes it possible to access particular content at any time one wants.
- *Regarding space*, it can be said that technically mediated communication is increasingly available at different localities, or is part of the construction of such localities. Ever more 'locations' are becoming 'media locations', while during movement between these places it is possible to access media. The telephone is no longer only a media technology linked to particular communicative places – the office, the home or a public phone box. The personal mobile phone can be used in any location. Much the same can be said for television, with a shift (again) out of the home to public viewing, whether in opens spaces or in publicly accessible premises, such as pubs.
- These examples relate to the *social dimension* of mediatization: that more and more social relationships and institutions are characterized by technologically mediated communication. To take a further example: the use of a computer is no longer linked only to work. Whether mailing, surfing or playing, the computer bridges the public and private social spheres, working hours and leisure time.

On the whole, there is a synergy in the increase of different media in human life. Partly because of this it is characterized by particular 'waves' or 'leaps', as, for example, when digitalization and cross-media content production fundamentally alter the use of media in very different contexts. This is yet another reason for refusing to treat the quantitative aspects of mediatization as part of a linear process.

But more important here is that this involves *qualitative aspects* of change. These qualitative aspects of mediatization can be understood if one considers more closely how technical media 'structure' the way in which we communicate; or, alternatively, how the way in which we communicate 'reflects' the technical changes of media. It is this reciprocal relationship that can be examined more closely once one turns to the question of the concrete forms taken by mediatization in divergent socio-cultural fields. I will deal with this in the following section.

Communication and the Moulding Forces of the Media

The qualitative aspects of the media dealt with so far can be characterized more precisely by the idea of the *moulding forces of the media* (Hepp 2009): media as such exercise a certain 'pressure' upon the way in which we communicate. The television is today, for example, associated with a 'pressure' to render certain ideas more 'visual'. To take another example, today's print media make possible the development of more complex arguments, including a greater number of elements, since they are used at a slower rate and governed by the preferences of the reader, unlike audiovisual media. And a final example: the mobile phone allows one to remain continuously connected with particular people, even when one is on the move – and the mobile tends to 'pressure' the individual to maintain such connectivity. Nonetheless, all of these examples show that we are not here talking about the 'direct effect' of the media's material structure. *The moulding forces of the media become concrete only in the process of media communication, depending on the form of appropriation in very different ways.* Among British writers this is referred to as the need for media to become 'domesticated' (Silverstone and Hirsch 1992; Berker et al. 2006; Hartmann 2006; Röser 2007).

The conception of the moulding forces of the media adheres therefore to points made in the previous chapter concerning Medium Theory: that there are specific features of particular media that we *also* need to take into account if addressing the issue of changes in communication. These specific features are, however, produced by people's activities, so that they are to a great extent contextual and do not suggest the presence of a particular media logic. We need to focus our attention on the contextuality of a many-layered process of transformation.

As Raymond Williams suggested in his classic text *Television: Technology and Cultural Form*, we need to treat media simultaneously as technology *and* cultural form. The point of such an approach is the avoidance of 'technological determinism', and also 'symptomatic technology'. Williams considers that the first treats the relationship between social change and technology as one driven by technology. In this approach new technologies emerge from an autonomous process of research and development and are made available to the public: '[N]ew technologies . . . create new societies' (Williams: 2003: 6). With symptomatic technology the problem is different, for technologies are an expression of ongoing social change. 'Any particular technology is then as it were a by-product of a social process that is otherwise determined' (2003: 6). Technologies affect social change 'but in a more marginal way' (2003: 6). Williams regards both approaches as inadequate, for they isolate media as technologies from ongoing social change: in the first case it emerges separately but then becomes a driving force; in the second the technology is dependent upon change but is in itself marginal to social change. These two approaches are contrasted with another:

It may be possible to outline a different kind of interpretation, which would allow us to see not only its history but also its uses in a more radical way. Such an approach would differ from technological determinism in that it would restore intention to the process of research and development. The technology would be seen, that is to say, as being looked for and developed with certain purposes and practices already in mind. At the same time the interpretation would differ from symptomatic technology in that these purposes and practices would be seen as direct: as known social needs, purposes and practices to which the technology is not marginal, but central. (2003: 7)

Quite remarkably, we can see in these thoughts of Williams clear parallels to Actor-Network Theory as developed by Bruno Latour. With Latour the context is of course different, since he is not concerned with questions of media technology, but rather how 'things', or 'objects' or, as he calls them, 'non-humans' are to be treated as part of the social (Latour 2007: 72). Like Williams, he seeks a path between the two poles of technological and social determinism. He differentiates himself from these as follows:

> It is fair to say that social scientists were not alone in sticking polemi-cally to one metaphysics among the many to hand. To avoid the threat of 'technical determinism', it is tempting adamantly to defend 'social determinism', which in turn becomes so extreme (the steam engine becoming, for instance, the 'mere reflection' of 'English capitalism') that even the most open-minded engineer becomes a fierce technical determinist bumping [*sic*] the table with virile exclamations about the 'weight of material constraints'. These gestures have no other effect but to trigger even a moderate sociologist to insist even more vehemently on the importance of some 'discursive dimension'. (Latour 2007: 84)

His own position seeks a path between these two extremes, treat-ing even technological 'things' as 'actors' (2007: 71). 'Objects', even when these are media technologies, are in 'chains which are association of humans ... and non-humans' (1991: 110). The core of Latour's argument is that these things are ultimately 'congealed actions' from human actors. A handrail is in a certain sense nothing other than the guarding action of a human who wants to protect somebody else from falling. It is for this reason that objects are themselves to be conceived as in 'associations' – in social connection – with actions as acting objects. To cite Latour once more: 'Social action . . . is also shifted or delegated to different types of actors which are able to transport the action further through other modes of action, other types of forces altogether. . . . [I]mplements, according to our definition, are actors, or more precisely, *participants* in the course of action waiting to be given a figuration' (Latour 2007: 70–1, emphasis in original). Latour ascribes to 'acting' 'things' the potential to power relations and inequalities by these kinds of reification. He seeks to investigate power and domination with the aid of 'the multiplicity of objects' by which they become 'empirically visible' (2007: 83). ANT as Actor-*Network* Theory gets its name from this approach to the treatment of 'things' as acting in networks, or in connectivity with other actors. The concept of network here is fuller than it usually is in the study of media and communications, since it is not a matter of social networks, but rather the networking of different actors and actions. As Joost van Loon puts it: 'ANT does not presuppose that order, or perhaps better continuity, is a reflection of some reality "out there", but instead that it is the consequence (a construction) of a (temporary) stabilization of a particular set of forces that can be conceptualized as a *network*' (Loon 2008: 114, emphasis in original).

If these ideas are applied to media, they become reconceivable as 'mediators'. Media are to be understood not as 'transparent' instances of communication, but rather as institutionalized *and* reified 'objects' that have moments shaping the process of communication. If one thinks of media as complex human actions that have 'congealed' into institutions and technological apparata, then Latour's reflections give us ways of thinking about the manner in which their 'specifics of mediation' can be dealt with analytically. As noted several times already, we are not here looking for the 'causal effect' of technology. Media are as such only conceivable in terms of human action, but they do reveal in their entirety a *particular potential for action*; this we can call the *moulding forces of media*, which become the object of our analysis. What Raymond Williams calls the 'purposes and practices already in mind' (2003: 7) that constitute the meaning of the development of the media as technology are, in the processes of their appropriation, 'modified'.

This understanding of the moulding forces of the media as a convergence of (i) the institutionalization and (ii) the reification of communicative action recalls some of the arguments developed by Berger and Luckmann in *The Social Construction of Reality*, but also clearly differs from them in other respects (see Knoblauch 2011). I understand *institutionalization* entirely in the sense used by Berger and Luckmann, not only as the habitualization of social action, but also as a reciprocal typification of habitualized actions by particular types of actors (1967: 72). An institution is thus, for example, the family, which typifies particular forms of action in terms of types of actors ('father', 'mother', 'current partner', 'child', 'aunt', and so forth). In this sense, using 'institution' when considering the media does not only mean media organizations, something which is implicit in Hjarvard's treatment of mediatization (even if media organizations are obviously *one form* of institutionalization). At stake are processes of institutionalization that are more far-reaching, such as mobile communications, which institutionalize a communicative triadic relationship (Höflich 2005): 'caller', 'called' and 'bystanders'.

While the concept of institutionalization maps on to that of social constructivism, there are differences in the process of reification. Berger and Luckmann talk in this regard of 'objectivation' (1967: 78). They mean by this that the institutional world 'objectifies' human activities, rendering them into phenomena independent of the individual. For Berger and Luckmann, language is a clear example of this, which is the reason they treat this as a first and decisive 'objectivation' of the human being. However, 'objectification', in their eyes, goes one step further, to 'reification': 'Reification is the apprehension of human phenomena as if they were things, that is, non-human or possibly supra-human terms.' In other words, 'reification is the apprehension of the products of human activity *as if* they were something other than human products' (1967: 106, emphasis in original; cf. also Berger and Pullberg 1965). Examples for this are facts of nature, results of cosmic laws, manifestations of divine will. Reification therefore occurs where social reality does not appear to have been 'constructed' by people, but appears as a 'given'.

The Mediatization of Culture

The concept of *reification* as it is used here involves a different emphasis. It is used to denote a particular form of objectivation, but only in the widest sense of a materialization in media technologies. In Latour's view there is a specific quality to this technological character which, for example, distinguishes it from language. For this reason it is important when dealing with media to talk of the moulding forces as the concurrency of institutionalization (which includes the objectivation of language) *and* reification (objectivation as a particular form of technological materialization). That is the reason why we need a special term for this: in the analysis of media we always have to think of both moments of objectivation together, without erasing their differences.

Even if there are differences here with social constructivism, there is another connection that should be emphasized. While there is no sense that in the everyday world media technologies appear to be the product of 'divine intervention', it is nonetheless true that some kind of autonomous power is *ascribed* by humans to media technologies: TV, computer games, emailing – all of these 'do' something to us. There is here an element of reification in the conceptual architecture of Berger and Luckmann. The architecture we have developed here is intended not to further this kind of essentialist approach, but instead to question and look beyond it. That is why emphasis has been laid upon the fact that the moulding forces of the media can only develop in the context of human action.

We also need to keep in view the idea that any one media technology is itself a 'bundle' of the most varied techniques, and is not a homogeneous apparatus. Ivan Illich, whom I cited in the Introduction, makes this extremely clear. Illich deconstructed the 'technology' of the printed book, indicating the presence of what were initially socio-cultural inventions in the course of its lengthy and complex genesis:

This breakthrough [of the printed book] consisted in the generalization of more than a dozen technical inventions and arrangements through which the page was transformed from score to text. Not printing, as is frequently assumed, but this bundle of innovations, twelve centuries

59

earlier, is the necessary foundation for all the stages through which bookish culture has gone since. (Illich 1993: 3–4)

Similar things can be said of other media technologies, for instance film, television or the Internet – in all of these cases there are diverse 'bundles of innovation' that come together into that which, at the end of the process of reification, comes to be known as a singular media technology. And so, much as with ANT, we find in Illich's comments on the book as a medium arguments regarding technological 'things' which direct our attention to the 'combination of those elements' (Illich 1993: 3) through which communicative action became reified in the materialization of particular media.

If this line of thought is applied to the previous argument concerning the *moulding forces of the media* it becomes plain that, likewise, we cannot describe the media technology of today in terms of specific features that a medium 'of itself' develops. In this sense the medium is certainly *not* the 'message'. *Nor* does the medium provide a 'massage', which Medium Theory partly suggests (see for example the title of the 1967 book by McLuhan and Fiore, *The Medium is the Massage*). The moulding forces of the media must always be studied as they interact with human action, especially (but not exclusively) with communicative action. Or, as it would be phrased by a media and communications research programme orientated to cultural theory: the moulding forces of the media are first articulated in their *appropriation* as a process of cultural localization (Hepp 2006: 248–63). Media, as reified and institutionalized frameworks formed out of a large number of (communicative) actions, become 'powerful' in interwoven practices; and this process is neither a causal one, nor autonomously given, but is realized through shaping actions. This is what marks out the concept of moulding forces. Media, as 'congealed complexes of interwoven actions', are fitted for varied purposes, and this potential first develops through a process of appropriation characterized by diverse practices which far exceed the customary idea of the 'use' of particular media (see Hasebrink 2003). This is exactly what a contextual investigation of the moulding forces of the media does.

If we take these ideas seriously, we then need to deal with the *concept of communication* in greater depth, developing the brief outline given in the Introduction. As already noted in the Introduction, by communication I mean any form of symbolic interaction either conscious and planned or habitualized and situated (for more detail on the concept of communication, see Reichertz 2009, 2011). By this I mean that communication depends upon the use of signs which humans learn during socialization and which, as symbols, are for the most part arbitrary, such that they are founded upon socio-cultural rules. Interaction means the people's mutually related social action. Here the concept of communication used in this book corresponds to the concept of communication used ever since ideas drawn from symbolic interaction theory began to be diffused in media and communication studies. Hence communication is the precondition of people's constitution of reality – we 'create' our own social reality in manifold communicative processes, although not exclusively so.

If we talk of communication as action, then it is important to highlight some specific aspects of (social) action as against simple behaviour. There is not the space here to engage in a discussion of Max Weber's (2013) theory of action as presented in the first chapter of *Economy and Society* (see, for example, Schütz 1967; Lenk 1978; Luckmann 1992), but it is I think necessary to raise a few points that will prevent later misunderstanding. The key difference between action and behaviour is that the first is 'meaningful' and 'purposive' action, or lack of action (*Unterlassen*), hence behaviour which is controllable and 'responsible' (Holly et al. 1984: 288). The concept of behaviour therefore describes more or less unreflected 'doing' (communicative praxis in respect of communication), whereas the concept of action relates to the completed deed (Luckmann 1992: 48). Action is based upon social rules that are acquired through socialization.

It is important to clarify this since it makes clear that treating communication as mutual action does *not* necessarily imply that characterizing communication as mutual action is fully captured in the concept of intentionality or *Verstehen* of this intention (for a critical assessment see Reichertz 2009). Most important is the question of manageability: 'If one understands action to be meaningful, one also implies that it is "purposive", but not that it also always has to be intentional, deliberate and conscious' (Holly et al. 1984: 289–90). In this sense the description of an action or a practice is always an 'interpretative construct' (Lenk 1978), hence an imputation from the position of an observer. Communication as action or practice is to a great extent habituated and, to use here a concept from Anthony Giddens (1984: 375), is exclusively 'practically conscious': people have the capacity to *act* in a communicatively appropriate manner. But they are not necessarily in a position to *express discursively* this practical knowledge of 'how to do communication'.

In many instances of communication it is not necessarily a case of achieving communicative contact or a follow-up communication, as is usually the case with a joint exchange of some kind of content. Communication is instead bound up with very much more extensive action or practice: roofers check with each other verbally while they are tiling a roof, clerks continue to ask questions while they are determining a sequence of events, and so on. Actual communicative action cannot be separated from networks of other action, both with and without media, with other things or without other things. It is for this reason that Jo Reichertz talks of communication being 'people's mutual orientation through symbolic means embedded in social practices' (2009: 98). And he goes on to argue that communication in particular involves a 'power of communication' (2009: 198) in the sense of Max Weber's concept of power (see Weber's *Economy and Society* Ch. 1 §16). For Weber, power is the chance that, within a given social relation, one will be able to enforce one's will even when meeting resistance, quite independently of the basis for this chance. Hence *power of communication* is the implementation of such a will through communication. However, one's 'will' should not be here understood to mean 'the conscious intention of acting with power'. As has been said, and made more precise here: very frequently the rules and patterns of powerful communicative action are very largely habituated. The concept of power of communication does not imply, as with the frequently used concept of 'effect', outcomes of media-mediated communication that can be measured more or less definitely. It is more open than this, because in Weber power *always* implies chance, and *never* certainty. Above all, this concept of power of communication relates to the social dimension of communication, so that ultimately the (disciplined) social relationship is considered to be the real source of power of communication. With some exaggeration, Reichertz formulates this as follows (cf. also Reichertz 2011):

> It exists – everyday power of communication which gets by without issuing commands, making threats or engaging in bribery. For the most part communication succeeds on an everyday basis without coercion (nor threat or bribery), but never without power. But this is a power that arises from the relations of actors one to another, and from the significance of the other for the determination of one's own identity. This power ultimately depends upon recognition, and hence upon voluntary free will. (Reichertz 2009: 242)

Questions of the power of communication become relevant in respect of the moulding forces of the media because the reification and institutionalization of particular communicative transactions in media lend particular forms of communicative power a lasting basis: in the creation of organizations and the construction of material communications infrastructure lasting probabilities of possible influence are created in communication. Classic examples of this are to be found in the usual mass media such as radio and TV, whose reification and institutionalization centre communication with one particular broadcaster, and so render permanent individual forms of communicative power as part of the moulding forces of these media. We can also find in the Internet similar forms through which communicative power is rendered permanent, as for instance in the way that social web providers like Facebook store data. The way in which such information is 'collected' and 'analysed' by providers making use of technical information structures secures communicative power. Such contextual processes of reification and hence extension are elements of the moulding forces of the media that require critical attention.

How do we now create some sort of systematic order in our treatment of media-mediated communication, and the moulding forces which are apparent in such media? We can return to some ideas of John B. Thompson's introduced at the beginning of this chapter and use them to extend our present argument. Thompson (1995: 82–7) has suggested, in relation to his discussion of mediatization, distinguishing three types of communication preceding the general spread of electronic mass media: face-to-face interaction; interaction mediated by media; and quasi-interaction mediated by media. If we also bring in here Krotz's work (2007: 90–2), there is a fourth type related to the last great surge of mediatization – the synergies of increasing digitalization of quite diverse kinds of communicative equipment – and this fourth type is communication as interaction with 'intelligent' or 'interactive systems'. Integrating the work of both authors, we can present the basic types of communication as shown in Table 3.2.

This systematization distinguishes four types of communication:

- firstly, as *direct communication*, i.e. direct conversation with other people;
- secondly, as *reciprocal media communication*: that is, technically mediated personal communication with other persons (for instance, through the use of a telephone);
- thirdly, as a *produced media communication*, characterizing the sphere of media communication classically identified by the concept of mass communication (newspapers, radio, TV);
- fourthly, *virtualized media communication*, by which is to be understood communication by means of 'interactive systems' created for this purpose – computer games are one example, and another would be robots.

This systematization generally make clear that, with reciprocal and produced media communication, the restriction of symbolic means by comparison with that prevailing under direct communication leads to the separation of the contexts of participating interacting agents. As a consequence the possibility arises of an extended access to communication across space and time. Technical media permit communication beyond the locality of direct relationship to become 'disembedded' (Giddens 1990: 21).

Table 3.2 Basic types of communication

	Direct communication	Reciprocal media communication	Produced media communication	Virtualized media communication
Constitution in time and space	Co-present context; shared system of space and time references	Separation of contexts; extended access to space and time	Separation of contexts; extended access to space and time	Separation of contexts; extended access to space and time
Range of symbolic means	Variety of symbolic means	Limitation of symbolic means	Limitation and standardization of symbolic means	Relative limitation and standardization of symbolic means
Action orientation	Orientated to specific others	Orientated to specific others	Orientated to an indefinite potential number of addressees	Orientated to a potential space of action
Mode of communication	Dialogical	Dialogical	Monological	Interlogical
Form of connectivity	Local	Translocally addressed	Translocally open	Translocally indefinite

Source: Own systematization based on Thompson (1995: 85) and Krotz (2007: 90–2).

Hence communication opens up translocal connectivities without there being any necessity of moving from one's locality; there is, as we say, a 'connection' beyond the local. This disembeddedness goes furthest in one particular sense in virtual media communication. Here potential spaces of action are opened up by media technologies, spaces which are then appropriated for the most varied communicative interaction in a quite indefinite way.

If we examine these relationships more closely, the following becomes plain: while *direct communication* occurs in a context of co-presence with a shared time–space reference system, this communication creating something like local connectivity, there is a difference with the translocal connectivity of *reciprocal media communication*. Here the use of technical media enables the participants to exist in contents that are separate in space and/or time. They therefore do not share a common reference system in the sense outlined above. This is exemplified in mobile phone conversations, in which there is an apparent necessity to first create a common reference system for the interacting partners through 'doubling of spaces' (Moores 2008: 194) – the creation of a shared 'space of talk'. In general, what is gained in such translocal communicative connectivity through the mediatization of communication is matched by a loss in symbolic means with which communication is, or can be, made. This can be called translocally addressed connectivity insofar as the translocal connectivity of reciprocal media communication remains related to specific interacting partners.

A further aspect of connectivity becomes evident with *produced media communication*. Here again this starts out translocal, since communication is here disembedded from its local context through the use of technical media. Produced media communication is directed to an indefinite potential set of others, in contrast to both reciprocal media communication and direct communication. Correspondingly the connectivity so established has to be understood differently, as a translocally open connectivity, or as a communication framework with blurred edges. The resulting gain in connectivity – the possibility of communicative connectivity to a large number of unspecified others – is again matched by a loss, since a dialogical communicative relationship is replace by a monological relationship. This is precisely the case with the classic mass media such as the newspaper, radio or TV, and also their digitalized versions – online newspapers, digital radio and Internet TV.

As I have already mentioned, the situation with *virtualized media communication* is more complex. To some extent the restriction of symbolic means is here a relative one, since there exist particular communication robots such as Sony's Aibo and similar equipment makes possible (once again) a great range of communication, for example, through gesture. Much the same is true of computer games. Nintendo's Wii uses movement sensors to transfer gestures into a virtualized space of action, for instance. We can even talk here of 'interlogue' intervening between the producers of interactive contexts and users of a virtual action space in which, from the point of view of the users, the real communicative action takes place. The connectivities arising here are correspondingly non-specific: while from the point of view of users the connectivity runs ultimately between user context(s) and the virtual action space, there is from a broader point of view another connectivity involved, arising from the production of these virtual action contexts and its appropriation.

Systematizations of this kind do not go unchallenged in the study of mediatization. Hjarvard (2008: 122) criticizes Thompson's original formulations (which are extended here), arguing that his distinction remains too closely linked to the differentiation of media-mediated personal communication and mass communication. Hjarvard proposes that a distinction should only be drawn between direct and media-mediated communication, following this with other distinctions, such as whether communication occurs one-way or two-way, on an interpersonal or mass basis, or through textual, auditory or visual means, and so forth. One can certainly agree that further distinctions of this kind are important for empirical analysis. Nonetheless, the kind of systematization attempted here has the potential to provide some degree of orientation in making further distinctions that are more closely related to the basic characteristics of communication in the era of mediatization. This seems important not least because of the quite diverse forms of institutionalization and reification in the power of communication: monologically produced communication, for example, implies the centralization of communicative power in the hands of a few; interlogic, by contrast, is associated with communicative power that rests in the possibility of creating virtual interaction spaces. But we have to be careful not to be too simplistic: as I will demonstrate later, empirical communication networks normally transgress the basic types of communication distinguished here.

Nevertheless, the systematization laid out here allows us to break down further still the panorama of mediatization. For a long time mediatization meant that new forms of reciprocal and produced media communication, with varying moulding forces, developed; now we can say that virtualized media communication has created a further impulse in the process of mediatization whose moulding potential remains very hard to judge.

Mediatization therefore deals with the process in which these diverse types of media communication are established in varying contextual fields and the degree to which these fields are saturated with such types. For each field we need to study the manner in which moulding develops, the kinds of changes in communication that occur and hence the way in which reality is constructed. Even if the contexts of change to which the concept of mediatization is addressed are often referred to as 'the media', one must keep in mind that this is only a shorthand way of referring to a complex *dialectical* relationship that is under consideration. At root this is a matter of communication and the question of how far changes in communication indicate the existence of socio-cultural changes. Media are no more and no less than the reification and institutionalization of this change of communication. Their potential lies in the way in which media 'alter' communication. If we talk of the moulding forces of the media, then we are employing a metaphor with whose aid we can grasp this dialectic.

4

Cultures of Mediatization and
Mediatized Worlds

In the previous chapter we proceeded to unravel, step by step, what we might understand by 'mediatization'. I sought to make clear that mediatization is more than simply the process of mediation through media. Of course, mediatization does not involve the permeation of a media logic, however that might be conceived. Mediatization is instead more a conceptual construct, like individualization, commercialization or globalization; and to be understood as a panorama of a sustained metaprocess of change. This metaprocess is no linear evolution, but rather a process in which there are several ruptures and contradictory moments. Nonetheless, it is possible to state generally what has characterized the metaprocess of mediatization in Europe, at least over the last few decades: as a gathering diffusion of different forms of reciprocal, produced and virtualized media communication. This diffusion is also characterized by the way that the moulding forces of media in different contextual fields – work, everyday life, religion, politics, and so forth – have developed in a form specific to each field.

This understanding of mediatization makes it possible to define media culture more precisely. As this chapter will demonstrate, by media culture we should understand mediatized culture, no more and no less. Or put more generally: media cultures are the cultures of mediatization, which becomes concrete in certain mediatized worlds. In support of this I will develop my argument as follows. First of all, I will present the conception of media culture on the basis of the concept of mediatization that has already been developed. This then serves as a foundation for the development and understanding of our contemporary mediatized worlds. Following this, I turn to present-day social and communicative networks. I conclude by asking what might characterize the communicative figurations of today's cultures of mediatization.

Media Culture as a Concept

As already outlined, it makes sense to treat *media cultures as cultures of mediatization*. By this I mean that media cultures are cultures *whose primary meaning resources are mediated through technical communications media*, and which are '*moulded' by these processes in specifically different ways*. 'Resources of meaning' here means 'media products' such as 'text', 'film' or 'website' to which we relate when we generate meaning in (media) communication. I refer here to 'meaning resources' since meaning is not located 'in the product', but rather arises with its appropriation.

Of course, no culture is mediatized to such an extent that *all* of its meaning resources are mediated by the media. Since the human being is a physical being, there will always be a part of its cultural production of meaning that remains 'direct', or at least 'not mediated by the media' (Reichertz 2008: 17). The qualification 'primary' is important here. If one understands mediatization as in the previous chapter, as the process in which our cultures are increasingly permeated – temporally, spatially, socially – by media communication which itself moulds in various and contradictory ways, there must have been, historically, some point at which cultures became so heavily permeated and moulded by media communication that this became – on an everyday level – constitutive for the way in which this form of culture was articulated. 'Life' in and with such cultures is henceforth unimaginable without media. This happens if media, working with other social institutions in a continuous process, become socially 'constructed' as the centre of the society (Couldry 2009: 437): what counts as 'important' is what can be seen on the news; the 'most important' friends and acquaintances are organized through the social web; 'relevant' historical events are filmed; anybody who is 'really important' becomes a TV and/or Internet celebrity; and so on. These discursive patterns, which assume a *social construction of media centrality*, are familiar to most people living in cultures of mediatization from their everyday life. Correspondingly, cultures of mediatization are not simply cultures that can be characterized by mediatization understood as an increasing quantitative diffusion and qualitative moulding by processes of media communication. Rather, one can add: in cultures of mediatization both elements are developed to such an extent that for them 'the media' is constructed as the instance whose meaning resources are primary – they constitute and construct the centre.

Since cultures of mediatization depend upon the communicative connectedness of media-mediated communication, they are necessarily translocal. The term *translocality* here is an analytic concept which highlights the particular features of media cultures. 'Locality' as a component of this concept lends emphasis to the fact that, even with progressive mediatization, the local world does not cease to exist. Independently of whatever the reach of the communicative connectivity of a locality might be, this does not change the fact that a person lives out life for the most part in a particular locality (Moores 2000). As a physical human being you have to be somewhere. And if we also conceive media as reification, as in the previous chapter, then the materiality of its appropriation – through a TV set, a WLAN router, a cable network – is also fixed to a particular locality. The prefix 'trans-' directs our focus from questions of the local to questions of connectivity, to the ways in which mediation by the media is realized. It is therefore also a question of what communicative relationships exist in cultures of mediatization, what their specificity and peculiarity might be. Related to this, on the one hand, the orientation of research to the translocal character of media cultures emphasizes the continuing relevance of the local, while, on the other, localities in cultures of mediatization are strongly connected with each other, both communicatively and physically.

This concept of translocality also has to do with a particular form of thinking about culture. Not long ago Jan Nederveen Pieterse (1995) distinguished between two possible concepts of culture: the territorial and the translocal. Territorial concepts of culture are inwardly orientated and endogenous, focused upon the organicity, authenticity and identity of culture. This therefore involves ideas of culture as a 'functional organism'. Translocal concepts, by contrast, are outwardly orientated and exogenous, focused on hybridity, translation and continuing identification. The image of culture is different, having a greater emphasis on the processual, and upon openness. If we talk of media cultures as translocal phenomena, this distinction leads us to view this phenomenon in terms of the processual and of openness: cultures of mediatization are more or less hybrid; there is a need within them for constant translation; the identities lived out in them are changing identifications. We must therefore be careful of associating unquestioningly the concept of media culture with the national cultures of territorial states.

Broadening our concept of media cultures as cultures of mediatization, we can borrow from Stuart Hall (1997: 222) and state that culture is the 'sum of the different classificatory systems and discursive formations' to which our production of everyday meanings relates. In the case of media cultures, this production of meaning in everyday life is mediatized in the sense already outlined, and hence is also translocal. As a consequence, media cultures are a form of *thickening of translocal classification systems and formations of the articulation of meaning*. These processes of the articulation of meaning are embodied in complex circuits, in which it is useful to distinguish at minimum the different levels of articulation of production, representation, appropriation, identification and regulation (Johnson 1986; du Gay et al. 1997; Hepp 2004: 187). Analysing media culture in these terms, we are concerned with the manner in which cultures of mediatization are manufactured (production), depicted (representation), lived (appropriation), how this relates to the work of identity (identification), together with the impact of political or governmental influence (regulation) upon this, and vice versa. Hence it makes little sense to restrict media cultures to particular media products, such as with 'television culture' (Fiske 1987) or 'film culture' (Harbord 2002). There are also other levels of the articulation of media culture that we need to keep in view (see on this Hickethier 2003, and the contributions in Saxer 1998, Pias 1999, together with Pias et al. 1999).

The concept of 'thickening' used here is taken from the work of the Swedish anthropologist Orvar Löfgren. He developed the term from his careful analysis of Swedish radio in the 1920s and its role in 'the thickening of the nation-state from an idea and a geo-political space into a cultural space . . .' (Löfgren 2001: 29). He employs the term 'thickening' because he wishes to draw attention to the increasing intensity with which numerous 'minor' everyday practices and routines – the way, for instance, that weather forecasts relate a transnational phenomenon (the weather) to a national space (2001: 19) – layer upon layer, constitute a national culture. Analysis of cultural thickenings thus involves the development of a perspective upon the 'micro-physics' (2001: 11) of the articulation of culture.

Finally, it is possible to view the 'sum' of classification systems and discursive formations that go to make up the production of meaning in a media culture as a given assemblage of cultural patterns. The expression 'pattern' makes clear that we are dealing here not with singular phenomena, but rather with typical 'styles' of thought, of discourses or practices. In other words, the concept of cultural pattern denotes a particular 'form' or a particular 'type'. Many of these cultural patterns are characteristic of very different cultures; they appear in one way or another in different media cultures. This is what is meant when it is said that media cultures blur into one another. Ultimately this 'fuzziness' is part of our definition of media cultures: the processes of communication upon which the mediation of media cultures is based are translocal, and so they pass through the most varied locations; media cultures are not walled off from each other, and for this reason are compelled to engage in an ongoing process of translation. Some examples from the everyday world of today's cultures of mediatization can illustrate this. There are elements in the basic structure of a French, British or German talkshow that they share in common. In the same way, all three cultures are overlaid with the transnational media culture of HipHop, which has particular French, British or German variants. All of these media cultures can nonetheless be distinguished by the *thickening* of a number of patterns that are in themselves not exclusive to any one media culture. The specific character of a media culture can be ascertained by taking a 'core' through its thickening – at least as a typification of the given pattern of this culture. The concept of 'thickening' hence seeks to deal with the problem that we have great difficulty in grasping the 'complexity' (Hannerz 1992) and dynamic of today's cultures of mediatization if we approach them in terms of a clear-cut either/or exclusivity. It is on the contrary precisely because of the translocal, technical-based mediation of media cultures that we need to deal with today's cultures of mediatization as multilayered strata of diverse cultural thickenings. If, however, these thickenings are placed in a comparative framework, it becomes possible to distinguish and describe media cultures, despite their lack of clear boundaries. There are many social phenomena that make up media cultures as specific thickenings of cultural patterns – youth scenes, social movements, communities of belief, as well as regions, nations or supranational entities such as the European Union.

These thoughts suggest that today's cultures of mediatization are characterized by a *globalization of media communication* precisely because of their mediatization. If we understand by globalization in general the multidimensional increase of world-wide connectivity – an argument put forward by the sociologist and communications specialist John Tomlinson in his book *Globalization and Culture* (1999) – then the globalization of media communication involves the multidimensional increase of world-wide *communicative* connectivity (Hepp 2004: 125–35). We can understand this as a metaprocess, as already outlined in the previous chapter. As with the metaprocess of mediatization, the globalization of media communication has no one-dimensional logic, such that finally we will all be in one big 'global village', or be subject to 'cultural homogenization', arguments with which Medium Theory is particularly associated (McLuhan 1962). By the same token, it is possible to identify specific elements of the cultural changes associated with globalization, as some of my comments have already suggested.

Néstor García Canclini, the Mexican-Argentinian writer on culture and communications, has argued that the most prominent cultural change brought about by globalization is deterritorialization: mediated by the process of globalization, there is an increasing loosening of the apparently natural relationship between culture and socio-geographical territory (1995: 229). But there are diverse processes of (re)territorialization that run counter to this.

García Canclini directs attention to elements that are important for further discussion of the question of the translocality of media cultures. We can say that particular elements of their translocality might be territorial, while others are deterritorial. The first applies to the media cultures of specific nation states, which as national media cultures relate ultimately to particular territorial spaces of communication. The second case, of deterritorial media cultures, applies to phenomena such as particular popular cultures that are not exclusive to any one territorial space of communication, and for whose articulation territory is not *constitutive* (whereas we also find that there are certain moments of territorialization, for example when a deterritorial popular culture like HipHop becomes nationalized). Translocality as an analytical category is of assistance here in directing our attention to the increase in connectivity transcending territorial boundaries that the globalization of media communication has brought about. In this respect the concept of translocal media cultures points to the existence of numerous cultural thickenings in the era of increasing mediatization and globalization.

Mediatized Worlds

An approach to media cultures in terms of a mediatization of culture transcending individual media – which is consequently transmedial – necessitates clarification that goes beyond the general points made so far. How should we go about empirical work on media cultures if we assume that the mediatization of culture takes different forms in different fields? How should we start, given that we have rejected the position of Medium Theory and so no longer consider 'TV' or 'the mobile phone' or 'the social web' to be the dominating medium of a certain historical phase? One possible way of answering these questions is to begin with specific 'mediatized worlds' (Krotz et al. 2008a). These provide a first approximation for everyday manifestations of media culture.

The study of media and communications has long talked of 'media worlds'. Altheide and Snow (1991), for example, characterize a 'media world' as a social world constructed in terms of a media logic. Elizabeth Bird (2003) has used an ethnographic perspective to describe the everyday use of (mass) media as 'living in a media world'. Faye D. Ginsburg, Lila Abu-Lughod and Brian Larkin (2002) characterize the (cultural) anthropology of the media as an ethnographic analysis of diverse cultural media worlds. Leah A. Lievrouw (2001) sees the establishment of 'new' digital media as in a functional relationship with a pluralization of life-worlds. Or David Morley talks in relation to the idea of belonging of 'our contemporary mediated world' (2001: 443). Similar ideas have been expressed in the German-language literature, the expression 'media world(s)' being common from the end of the 1980s at the latest (see, for example, Sander and Vollbrecht 1987; Baacke et al. 1991). The term 'media worlds' has therefore become an accepted one in media and communication studies. Insofar as this usage is anything more than metaphorical, then Alfred Schütz's social phenomenology is a central point of reference. (For a general assessment of the notion of the 'everyday', see the contributions in Thomas 2008 and Röser et al. 2009.) Therefore, I now want to turn to Schütz's propositions, relating them to the foregoing characterization of media culture as a mediatized culture.

In his posthumously published book *The Structures of the Life-World*, which he wrote with Thomas Luckmann (Schütz and Luckmann 1973), Schütz used a 'phenomenology of the mundane' to 'register the most general basic features of the life-world' (Hitzler and Eberle 2003: 110). This involved a '*proto*-sociological enterprise which provided a foundation for actual sociological work' (Hitzler and Eberle 2003: 110, emphasis in original). Prominent here was an 'epistemological clarification' (Hitzler 2007: 86) of the manner in which a subjective orientation to the world resulted in the meaningful construction of the social world. Central to this definition of the 'structures of the life-world' is the conception of the everyday life-world, or, more simply, the everyday world. In the view of Schütz and Luckmann, the everyday life-world is 'that province of reality which the wide-awake and normal adult simply takes for granted in the attitude of common sense' (1973, Vol. 1: 3). The everyday life-world is accepted without question, not the 'private world' of individual(s), but intersubjectively: '[T]he fundamental structure of its reality is shared by us' (1973, Vol. 1: 4). Hence everyday life includes not only 'nature' as experienced by the individual, but also the 'social (and therefore cultural) world in which I find myself' (1973, Vol. 1: 5). The protosociology of phenomenology seeks to reveal the 'structuredness of the life-world for the living subject' (1973, Vol. 1: 15).

If we take into consideration the work of Michel Foucault (1991) on the social mediation of the subject (see Thomas 2009), we might be cautious in accepting the claim that the structures of the life-world elaborated by Schütz and Luckmann provide us with a universal conceptual apparatus (see Reichertz 2009: 66–9). But even if we share this scepticism, Schütz and Luckmann give us an important point of departure for understanding more clearly what mediatized worlds are. Schütz has in fact prompted a widespread interest in contemporary socio-cultural manifestations of today's everyday world. Here we are concerned less with developing the conceptual apparatus of phenomenology as a protosociology than with with engaging in social-scientific analysis.

Benita Luckmann pointed out a long time ago (1970) that the everyday life-world was disintegrating into various 'small life-worlds', as she called them. She treats these as 'sectors of everyday life', consisting of both private and institutional contexts. These small life-worlds as 'socially constructed part-time realities' (Hitzler and Honer 1984: 67) increasingly characterize people's experience in contemporary cultures and define the 'multidimensional nature of everyday life' in these cultures. If we take up this point of Ronald Hitzler's (2008b), we gain an insight into the process of individualization in modern societies that is relevant here: the increasing

potential, and obligation, to choose between different lives is associated with the increasing variety of small life-worlds:

> Small social life-worlds are separate and structured fragments of the
> life-world, within which experiences arises in relation to special and
> mandatory given intersubjective caches of knowledge. Small social
> life-worlds imply a subjective experience of reality in partial, or part-
> time, cultures. These worlds are 'small' not because they only occur in
> limited domains, or have only a limited number of members. They are
> instead referred to as 'small' because within them the complexity of
> possible relevance is reduced to a specific hierarchy and system of rele-
> vance. We call these small life-worlds 'social' because these systems of
> relevance are intersubjectively obligatory for successful participation
> . . . . (Hitzler 2008b: 136)

Hitzler is himself especially interested in one form of small life-
worlds, 'event-worlds'. These are distinguished by the fact that
within them the subjective experience in the stream of consciousness is marked out as 'extra-ordinary' (Hitzler 2008b: 135). One
prominent example is that of event-worlds arising from participation in diverse events, something with which we are all confronted
today (Hitzler 2000). The extra-ordinary nature of these event-
worlds is fostered by 'multifarious 'vehicles' for consumption',
among which 'technical media' are central: 'Books, radio, television, films, the Internet and so on' (Hitzler 2008b: 135).

I want to take up the point that Hitzler makes here about the
media in event-worlds and refer it to 'small life-worlds' in general.
We can assume in media cultures that the various small life-worlds
are *in total* articulated in relation to media, whether these are small
life-worlds in public life (related to education, work, politics, and
so forth) or in private life (related to leisure, family or neighbourhood, for example). Where reference is made below to *mediatized
worlds*, this should be understood to involve mediatized social
worlds of the 'small life-world' kind. These are characterized anal-
ogously to the concept of media culture developed in the previous
section, as *mediatized* worlds, since *the resort to communications
media is constitutive for the articulation of these social worlds in
the present form.*

Based on this concept we can specify the statement that media cultures are manifested in different mediatized worlds in the following way: from the subjective standpoint of a person, cultures of mediatization in their variety become tangible as complexes of mediatized worlds. Here the manner of mediations varies from one mediatized world to the other. While for the mediatized worlds of some families it is typically the TV, mobile phone, email, chatroom, social web and computer games that are characteristic, for other families these worlds are characterized by TV, radio, newspapers and cinema. The *task* of empirical research into media cultures is to typify these relationships. If we recognize that today's media cultures get concrete in very different mediatized worlds, then it becomes clear how difficult it can be to identify general tendencies in cultures of mediatization. We can interpret in this way Hitzler's statement that 'the concept of "mass culture" is in no respect adequate to describe experienced social reality and the schemata of meaning and expression that mould them' (2008b: 136).

If we go further in defining such mediatized worlds, then we could also make use of symbolic interactionism. The idea of a 'world' is widespread here too, although more in the form of a 'social world'. This concept was first introduced by Thomas Shibutani (1955). Even though he in no respect argues on the ground of a sociophenomenology, he is interested in much the same thing as Benita Luckmann: the number of different social worlds that make up modern societies. From the viewpoint of media and communication studies the following idea is of relevance: for Shibutani, each social world 'is a culture area, the boundaries of which are set neither by territory nor by formal group membership but by the limits of *effective communication*' (1955: 566, emphasis added).

It is precisely this idea of communicative mediation that can be usefully incorporated into the conception of a mediatized world advanced here. Even at this early conceptual stage Shibutani notes a specific feature of social worlds in modern societies which he closely associates with the diffusion of produced media communication: because of the 'the development of rapid transportation and the media of mass communication, people who are geographically dispersed can communicate effectively' (1955: 566). For that reason, what we would call the contemporary mediatized worlds have multiplied, and no longer coincide with the social world of a reference group in any *one* particular locality or territory:

> Culture areas are coterminous with communication channels; since communication networks are no longer coterminous with territorial boundaries, culture areas overlap and have lost their territorial bases. Thus, next-door neighbors may be complete strangers; even in common parlance there is an intuitive recognition of the diversity of perspectives, and we speak meaningfully of people living in different social worlds – the academic world, the world of children, the world of fashion. (1955: 566)

Shibutani also notes that these worlds vary in stability and range of communicative possibilities according to their composition, size and spatial extent. He suggests that 'every social world has some kind of communication system . . . in which there develops a special universe of discourse . . .' (1955: 567). Above all, social worlds are not static phenomena, but subject to an ongoing process of communicative reconstitution: 'Worlds come into existence with the establishment of communication channels; when life conditions change, social relationships may also change, and these worlds may disappear' (1955: 567).

It is true that this understanding of social worlds remains imprecise, since the boundary between 'social world' and 'reference group' is not at all clear (see Strübing 2007: 81). Nonetheless, Shibutani's work remains of importance to an analysis of mediatized worlds for two main reasons. The first is the reference to communication processes, and the second the allusion to the mediality of communication. It is worth pursuing this line of thought in the work of the American sociologist Anselm Strauss (1978).

There are three emphases in the way that Strauss developed these ideas relevant to the study of mediatized worlds. Firstly, Strauss noted that the concept of social worlds 'might provide a means for better understanding the processes of social change' (1978: 120). This idea is already evident in Shibutani, where he points to the way in which social worlds have altered in the course of modernity. Secondly, Strauss makes clear that social worlds can be 'studied at any scale' (1978: 126), from the very smallest social world of local groups to the very largest or most extensive, and that work should be directed 'across many scales'. From this he proceeds to the way in which different social worlds nonetheless intersect on a broad scale with other social worlds: some worlds having sub-worlds; others interleaving with each other because people have membership in different social worlds. In his opinion this fits with his idea that these social worlds are highly fluid (1978: 123), thus breaking down the classical distinction between micro and macro analysis. Thirdly – and here Strauss differs clearly from Shibutani – he emphasizes that the concept of social world makes it possible to connect different forms of communication with 'palpable matters' (1978: 121). Among these are activities, sites, technologies and organizations that are typical of a particular social world.

These ideas can be linked to arguments presented above regarding the concept of communication, where, on the one hand, communication is embedded in multiple further social practices, while, on the other, we need to take account of institutionalization and reification through media technologies. The 'social world perspective' (the title of Strauss's 1978 essay) consequently points in the same direction as the arguments made above. Here Strauss introduces another concept for the description of social worlds and their interrelationship, that of 'arena' (1978: 124; 1993: 226). He argues that in each social world 'various issues are debated, negotiated, fought out, forced and manipulated by representatives of implicated subworlds' (1978: 124). The concept of 'arena' is also a 'scaleable conception' (Strübing 2007: 93) equally applicable to family conferences and institute meetings as to media debates or global media events. 'Arenas' are therefore closely linked to questions of media communication, and one can talk of 'social world media', each of which is characteristic of a social world and its relationship with others: 'Social world media are full of such partially invisible arenas' (Strauss 1978: 124).

These considerations from Strauss provide us with important elements which enable us to reformulate the conception of a mediatized world developed above. We can summarize this as follows:

81

- The reciprocity of media communicative and socio-cultural change – reflected by the concept of mediatization – can be expressed as a *description of changing mediatized worlds*. If there is such a reciprocity, we can study it by investigating the changes of specific mediatized worlds, or the changes in the intersections of diverse mediatized worlds.
- We need to view mediatized worlds as being of quite different *scales*. Such differences can be quite limited in extent or internal differentiation, but quite comprehensive all the same. To be explicit: 'small' in respect of the understanding of mediatized worlds developed involves not simply 'range', but also the reduction of complexity in relevant elements which especially results from a thematic reduction. Examples of this are the mediatized world of a social movement, a religious community or a social scene.
- The concept of a mediatized world does not imply that this world is articulated purely through communication; rather this arises from its *interlocking* with related technologies (which as apparatus and machinery have a particular physical presence) as well as other forms of action, with particular sites and organizations. We are dealing with *mediatized* worlds when the articulation of these social worlds depends upon different forms of media-mediated interaction, and thus represents a subjective manifestation of media culture.
- Mediatized worlds have *characteristic communicative arenas* which link themselves together in the general whole of this mediatized world. These communicative arenas are transmedial, but they also can include different forms of direct communication. Correspondingly, the description of mediatized worlds always involves a definition of their communicative arenas, which must be studied both in respect to their transmedial nature and in relation to further action and other aspects of the manifestation of this mediatized world.

To sum up, we can on this basis employ the conception of a mediatized world as a pragmatic starting point for the description of today's cultures of mediatization at the level of the everyday world. While a comprehensive description of media cultures is a nearly impossible undertaking, the conception of a mediatized world provides a point of departure for empirical study. For example, the mediatized world of everyday working life in bureaucracies could be studied; or that of the school; of a social scene; or of families and domestic partners. By studying such specific mediatized worlds we can, step by step, arrive at a comprehensive understanding of today's cultures of mediatization.

Networks of Communication and of the Social

At this point there is a valid question to be raised: how can the differing communicative arenas of mediatized worlds be analytically described? For this we do of course need a number of conceptions and categories. Many of them can only be developed in the course of empirical analysis, seeking to avoid a deductive approach to the rapidly changing mediatized worlds of present-day media culture. From the point of view of media and communication studies, however, the following is of greatest importance: what descriptive construct is available for comprehending the different forms of (media) communication that interlock in the arenas of mediatized worlds? For this I propose the analytical concept of communicative network, which can be clearly distinguished from the concept of social network.

This takes us into metaphors of connectivity to which I have previously referred (Hepp 2008). Generally, the expression 'connectivity' – as we have seen in relation to the different types of (media-mediated) interaction put forward by John Thompson – implies 'relations' or 'connections' of quite diverse character. The conception of connectivity is firstly a way of generally describing the formation of communicative relations of quite different type and range (see Tomlinson 1999: 3–10). This is open-ended, and so there are no necessary *consequences* implied by these communicative relationships. Communicative connectivities can be created both by reciprocal (email or telephone) and by produced media communication (with the world-wide web or TV). They can involve the reciprocities of an 'understanding', or involve 'political legitimation', but also multiple 'conflicts' or 'displacements'. It is precisely this which dictates the need to proceed with contextual sensitivity.

There are two ways of approaching an investigation of this kind, and each needs to be clearly distinguished, at the heuristic level at least. The first emphasizes structural aspects, while the second places the emphasis upon processual aspects. The first can be associated with the conception of *communication network*, while the latter describes *communication flows*, the processual consequences of communicative action. The conception of communicative networks seeks to identify more or less lasting structures of communication. Here we can translate Castells' conception of *social* networks into one of *communications* networks. These latter would then be 'open structures, able to expand without limits, integrating new nodes as long as they are able to communicate within the network, namely as long as they share the same communication codes (for example, values or performance goals)' (Castells 2000: 501).

This quote first of all makes plain that communication networks are articulated in terms of specific codes. Structures of communication do not simply exist, but are (re)articulated in a continuous communication process: communication networks always refer to the flow of communicative practice which constitutes them. Communication networks are far from being closed to each other, for one and the same person can be part of several different communication networks – this is a presupposition of the sheer variety of behavioural practice. A youth with a migrant background can be part of the communication network of a local clique, also part of a deterritorial network of a diaspora, as well as of the centralized communicative network of certain national mass media.

These remarks help us to understand what is meant by the expression 'node'. Heuristically, a node is a point at which communicative connectivities cross. At first glance this might seem an irritating formulation. Nonetheless, it does help us to take note of the important point that 'nodes' can, within communication networks, be very different things, and that this concept is – again – scalable: reciprocal media communication is a process of the production of a particular kind of connectivity in which speaking persons are the central 'nodes'. But 'nodes' can assume other social forms. For example, local groups can be described as 'nodes' in the communication network of a larger social movement or social scene; or one might describe the local affiliates in the communication networks of translational companies as 'nodes'. In such cases it is once again a matter of the communicative connectivity of produced media communication, through which a wider horizon of meaning of (local) groups or institutions is created, which themselves are in turn characterized by internal (media-mediated) interaction. Communication networks can be identified as working at entirely different levels – and it is for that reason that the conception opens up the chance of treating and comparing communication structures *across different levels*.

All the same, one should *not* assume that communication networks map on to social networks one-to-one if we wish to understand the latter as lasting social structures (Holzer 2006: 74–9). As *communication* structures, communication networks have an importance in themselves, referring in this way to the existence of a *diversity* of social networks. An example would be advertising for a product such as the iPod or iPad, whose structures can be reconstructed as transmedial communication networks but which do not really correspond to any social network (see Knoblauch 2008: 84f.) Conversely, we can assume not only that there is the communicative network of a 'brand community' of Apple fans (Pfadenhauer 2008: 217), but also that we can here see a close reciprocal relationship between social and communicative networks.

Hence emphasis is placed on the fact that the conception of a communication network makes it possible to deal with the communicative connectivity of mediatized worlds in a transmedial manner. We can relate the concept of a communication network to basic forms of communication which have already been distinguished (see Table 3.1), each of which is characterized by *different basic structures* of possible (partial) communication networks.

The communicative connectivity of *direct communication* is therefore characterized by the fact that this happens locally. We are thus able to understand the local connectivity of direct communication as a structure, at a particular site and at a particular time, if we analyse it in terms of the different structural mouldings of communication networks. Here we can make use of work by the American social scientist Harold J. Leavitt in the 1950s (Leavitt 1951: 39). He studied experimentally the complete structure of communicative networking in a group of five persons (in which each is networked communicatively with all others) and arrived at 'four communication networks' of differing 'degrees of centralization' (Mann 1999: 56) (see Figure 4.1). In solving a group task, group members were permitted to communicate only in writing within the network structure. The wheel structure is a centralized communication network, in which one person formed the centre. The circle structure is by comparison entirely decentralized. The 'Y' structure has limited centralization. The row structure centralizes communication sequentially. In the related experiment it turned out that those who communicated in a circular structure had the greatest level of satisfaction, but that a centralized network 'solved problems more quickly and accurately than a less centralized network' (Mann 1999: 58).

The degree to which such experiments lend themselves to generalization is, however, always very limited. Nonetheless, there are clear potentialities here for the application of this kind of analysis to communications structures. This becomes even clearer if one takes account of the fact that such considerations can be transferred to *reciprocal media communication*. Characteristic of these forms of communication is the fact that they can be addressed translocally, communication networks transcending any one location. It does have to be recognized here that the five-person structure described represents a stark simplification. In the 'real life' of existing mediatized worlds and their arenas of communication, we have to deal with much more complex networks of reciprocal media communication, consisting of many more members and whose structures can alter situationally in their technical mediation: And so while, for example, one deals with

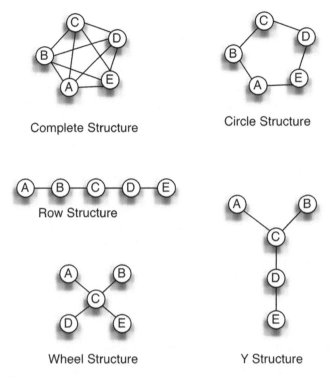

Figure 4.1 Communication networks in direct communication
based on Leavitt (1951: 39); Mann (1999: 57)

particular topics among a group of persons with whom one is in communication in a more or less egalitarian fashion and according to a complete structure (sending an email to anybody in this group), when making particular decisions within the same group one might select a Y structure: a small group having a preliminary discussion and then informing the wider group.

If we consider *produced media communication*, then the nodes of this kind of network are not just individual human beings. It can be said that the classical mass media, such as the TV, the newspaper or the radio (and the dissemination of all of these through the Internet), represent a highly centralized communication network. Their hub is formed by the organizations (or groups of persons) which offer produced contents, and with which a range of other people or groups of people are communicatively 'connected'. Here we come back to the point already raised above, that media as technologies permit specific relations of communicative power to be rendered enduring through their reification. The traditional mass media entrench their communicative networks by their embodiment in broadcasting institutions, radio masts, cables, and so on, and this in turn entrenches the power of their communicative structures. In addition, one can also see a form of reification in particular types of software code that, for example, secure the web pages of an online newspaper to ensure that particular discussions can only occur in specific communications fora, whereas the 'principal' content is supplied by the editorial team. This reified communication power creates potentialities, but also hierarchies and relations of dependency in communication networks. One potentiality would be the critical data journalism that has emerged in the last few years, evaluating sources of data available through the Internet sometimes on an automatized basis. Here we find new possibilities of critical investigation, where, for example, the movement of military units is reconstructed, so enabling official announcements by the military to be questioned. But hierarchies and relations of dependence remain in this respect: particular widespread 'stories' require dissemination in the classical mass media if they have any hope of being accessible to wider groups of people. For instance, the revelations of WikiLeaks became widely known for the first time when they were reported by the *Guardian*, the *New York Times* and *Der Spiegel*.

Remarkably, this perspective upon communicative connectivity also permits analysis of the modes of computer-mediated communications, following the work of Merrill Morris and Christine Ogan (1996). They compared different modes of computer-mediated communication according to temporal criteria (synchronous versus asynchronous) and also according to relationship structure (one-to-one, one-to-few, one-to-many, many-to-many). Morris and Ogan were chiefly interested in systematizing the various communicative possibilities of the Internet. In their schema, email is, for instance, an asynchronous one-to-one or one-to-few form of communication (and, having spam-mails in mind, we could also say: one-to-many form of communication), Skype is synchronous but with a one-to-one or one-to-few relationship structure, while an online newspaper communicates asynchronously one-to-many.

The relationship structure can, however, be understood much more clearly through a description of distinct communication networks, starting with the smallest complete structure, 'one-to-one', moving via various group structures right up to 'many-to-many' communication networks. It is not just a matter of what communicative possibilities are in general offered by email, Skype or online newspapers. We need to consider in addition how, in particular contexts, communication networks can be built up and maintained using these media. It might, for instance, be quite usual in some contexts to email synchronously, answering each mail immediately, as if one were chatting. By dealing with specific communication networks we can form a far more differentiated perspective than the rather crude framework offered by Morris and Ogan. As the examples show, we always need to bear in mind the way communication networks operate in terms of time. We need to take account of the degree to which particular communications networks are used in real time, or with a temporal lag.

Finally, we can relate the concept of *virtualized media communication* to communication networks. It can be said that, for example, particular computer games form technically a specific space of communicative networking, with avatars of other players or those driven by computer software. Quite how such a communication network can take shape is to some extent pre-programmed in the software, but from the translocal point of view it remains undetermined, since it is the appropriation of these possibilities that *de facto* constitutes the existing communication network. This can here only be a matter of the communication relationship of a player to an avatar managed by software, or the use of the game environment of an online game to create a communication network among players. Here again the forms of reciprocal media communication become an issue, if, for example, the game environment is used for chat. While it was for a long time assumed that these kinds of communication were only typical of younger people, more recently this has become part of the repertoire of older generations (Quandt et al. 2009).

These examples should serve to clarify the way in which a consideration of communication networks allows us to gain insight transmedially, beyond a consideration of individual media to the communicative articulation of mediatized worlds. The moulding forces of individual media have to be taken into account here, since the differing potentialities and restrictions implicated in the construction and maintenance of communication networks are capable of reinforcing an enduring communication power. This has to be seen as a potentiality, and one cannot meaningfully talk of one and the same medium – free of any context – 'constraining' a certain communication network. This also goes for the traditional mass media, especially if one recalls that their communication networks were not necessarily of the 'sender–receiver' type. In the early years of radio, Bertolt Brecht (1979, originally 1932) had already studied these potentialities. One of the arguments he developed was that radio, as a means of communication, also presented the possibility of stronger reciprocal communication. Additionally, we need to bear in mind that the communication networks of the classical mass media do not end at the 'receiver'. Elihu Katz and Paul Lazarsfeld showed in their 1955 study *Personal Influence* that we need to think in terms of a 'two-step flow' of communication. The communicative relationships embodied in mass media are bound into many other communication relationships of (mediatized) interaction, and we need to include these too in our analysis: for events which are taken up by the media are passed on, negotiated, assessed and criticized in everyday conversations. This is true not only of opinion leaders, who formed the axis of the earlier research, but of all of us (Keppler 1994; Hepp 1998). Ultimately, and from the perspective of the study of media and communications, any analysis of today's mediatized worlds has to relate them to transmedial communication networks.

Here we need to come back to a point raised before: that communication networks have no independent existence in themselves, but are continually created by people's communicative activity. Networks are a process, the consequence of the flow of communicative action in which communication networks articulate themselves over time. This perspective also reveals the situational character of communication networks. This has been demonstrated especially clearly by the media ethnographer Andreas Wittel (2008), even though he does not make a systematic distinction between communicative and social networks. Wittel is primarily interested in the investigation of a particular form of sociality which he dubs 'network sociality' and locates in particular in London's 'New Economy' of around 2000. He argues that this form of sociality is not based upon enduring narratives of shared experience; it is more informational. It is a matter of creating social networks which are to some extent separated out from other contexts and which serve, or are intended to serve, reciprocal needs. Their primary function is to furnish information on the current activity of another person, or other persons.

'Network sociality' is in this way based upon an ongoing networking practice whose nature is largely unknown. Using the concepts we have already developed, we can understand this as the processual construction or maintenance of complex networks of (media) communication. Examples cited by Wittel are network events like 'First Tuesday', where those local to the 'New Economy' meet. These can be treated as events of communicative networking, having 'the same function as a "medieval fair": they are about exchange' (Wittel 2008: 164), in this case of course it being (contact) information that is being traded. Other examples would be the organization of individual communication networks through databases with the intention of maintaining an instrumental social network. Another would be the private organization of dinner parties using email, connecting people situatively who did not know each other, but who the host thought had similar interests.

Analyses of this sort highlight two things. First of all, it becomes quite clear how much effort goes into the construction and maintenance of communication networks. These networks are not simple givens; they are articulated in the process of communicative action and have to be studied as such processes. The examples provided show the extent to which the moulding forces of media are bound up with sequences of activity. None of the local events would be conceivable without the use of computerized communication or databases for their organization. The actual form of the database also moulds how contacts are sorted. Secondly, it becomes evident that careful analysis of communicative networks is a necessary precondition for the understanding of social networks. Of course, the social networks of those associated with the London 'New Economy' do not map directly on to situative or monetary communication networks. But without their analysis it is hardly possible to come to grips with the mediatized world of the 'New Economy' at all. Hence we can read Wittel's analysis as a first attempt at empirically describing this kind of mediatized world.

Communicative Figurations

There is a question that follows from the argument presented so far. If we understand mediatized worlds as the everyday manifestation of media culture, and if we assume that, from the standpoint of media and communication studies, these can be analysed in terms of the communication networks underlying them, then we need to explain the following: how can we describe as a whole the various communication networks of a mediatized world, and possibly of cultures of mediatization? To do this I think we need the concept of communicative figuration, which can be developed from the work of Norbert Elias, already introduced above. This concept seems appropriate here because of its direct link to a theory of connectivity of the kind just developed.

According to Elias, figurations are 'networks of individuals' (1978: 15) which constitute a larger social entity through reciprocal interaction – through, for example, joining in a game, or a dance. This entity can be a family, a group, the state or society; in all of these cases these social entities can be described as different, complex networks of individuals. In taking this approach Elias seeks to avoid the idea 'that society is made up of structures external to oneself, the individual, and that the individual is at one and the same time surrounded by society yet cut off from it by some invisible barrier' (1978: 15). For Elias, 'individual' and 'society' are closely related and cannot be separated the one from the other. They involve two aspects of a whole which the concept of figuration is meant to identify. Figuration is therefore, according to Elias, a 'simple conceptual tool' (1978: 130) to be used to understand socio-cultural phenomena in terms of 'models of processes of interweaving' (1978: 130). If we take a game as our example, then a figuration describes 'the changing patterns created by the players as a whole' (1978: 130). This concept of figuration can be scaled in a fashion similar to the concept of a mediatized world. It will be helpful to cite Elias at length on this:

> [T]he concept of figuration ... can be applied to relatively small groups just as well as to societies made up of thousands or millions of independent people. Teachers and pupils in a class, doctor and patients in a therapeutic group, regular customers at a pub, children at a nursery school – they all make up relatively comprehensible figurations with each other. But the inhabitants of a village, a city or a nation also from figurations, although in this instance the figurations cannot be perceived directly because the chains of interdependence which link people together are longer and more differentiated. Such complex figurations must therefore be approached indirectly, and understood by analysing the chains of interdependency. (1978: 131)

The concept of figuration is accordingly intended to render social entities as processual phenomena of interrelation accessible to empirical analysis. In so doing we might clarify what really binds people together (cf. Elias 1978: 132).

These thoughts permit us to talk of *communicative figurations* as patterns of processes of communicative interweaving. Hence it can be said that a single communication network already constitutes a specific communicative figuration: this involves interwoven communicative action articulated in (mediatized) interaction. It is, however, of far greater interest to relate the concept of communicative figuration to the communication networks of different mediatized worlds as a whole. And so, for instance, the mediatized world of a social scene can be understood as being manifested in a particular figuration of communication networks. In the same way, the mediatized world of the culture of a diaspora can be identified with a characteristic communicative figuration, or one can talk of the communicative figuration of the mediatized world of a European public sphere, and so forth.

If communication networks are viewed as part of larger communicative figurations, then it is important that we do *not* regard them in an isolated manner and describe them individually, as tends to happen in the structural analysis of networks. Rather, we need to examine how *different* communication networks interlink with each other in the articulation of a specific mediatized world.

Communicative figurations are for the most part transmedial. A communicative figuration is very seldom based upon only *one* medium; usually it is based upon *several*. Examples would be: for the communicative figuration of families, a figuration which is increasingly scattered translocally, the (mobile) telephone is just as important as the social web, (digital) photo albums, letters, postcards or watching TV together. If we take (national or transnational) public spheres as communicative figurations, it is quite easy to see that these are constituted by a range of different media. That is not only a matter of the classical media of mass communication, but also of WikiLeaks, Twitter and blogs, together with the media of the social web. We also need to deal with the communicative figurations of social organizations: for instance, where social agencies, databanks, Internet portals as well as flyers and other PR media interrelate in seeking to reorganize and reorder different domains of the social – from pre-school education to post-retirement employment. Change in mediatized worlds demonstrates clearly the existence of change in communicative figurations which 'materialize' in different media.

This can be seen clearly in a study that we have conducted on the mediatization of migrant communities (Hepp et al. 2012). The purpose of this study was to analyse communicative networking among the Moroccan, Russian and Turkish diasporas in Germany by examining diverse media and forms of interaction. Using the concepts developed here, it can be said that the aim of the study was to identify the communicative figurations of diasporas. Here the communication networks of direct communication play a role, since the communicative networking of migrants takes place locally, through family conversations, meetings of clubs and associations and other events. But beyond this there is also reciprocal media communication that does not occur in one local place, but is conducted through (mobile) telephone, letters, email or (video) chatrooms, connecting to relatives in the home country, to other migrants of the same background, to migrants of other backgrounds in Germany and abroad. All of this must also be comprehended in terms of communication networks based upon produced media communication: the connection to the German-language area through TV (to learn the language), or access to the produced contents of the home country through satellite TV, Internet radio or (online) newspapers, through which access to the corresponding communication network in the home country is maintained. Finally, we have found that virtualized media communication in the form of computer games is of importance at least among younger migrants.

In this way we can show that such a complex communicative figuration of diaspora can be understood as a *co-articulation* of communicative networking and cultural identity within media appropriation. Through this study we have been able to distinguish three types of such a co-articulation: the 'origin-orientated', the 'ethno-orientated' and the 'world-orientated'. Put simply, it can be said that *origin-orientated* persons have a subjectively felt sense of belonging to their region of origin which moulds the life 'abroad'. This orientation is related to the kind of communicative networking that we have called 'origin networking'. Although there is intensive local communicative connectivity where they actually live, mostly with members of their own diaspora, there are also translocal communicative connections with their home regions. Those who are *ethno-orientated* behave differently. The term used to name them makes clear that their sense of belonging is located between the country of origin and the national context in which they live. Their communicative networking can be described as bicultural, since they are both local and translocal in relation to two (imagined) national cultures: that of the country of origin, and the country to which they have migrated. A third form of co-articulating cultural identity and communicative networking is typical of those who are *world-orientated*. This idea of orientation to the wider world highlights the way in which their sense of cultural belonging goes beyond the national level, at whatever level this might be. Conceptions of the nation – whether that of Germany, the country of origin or something between the two – are transcended, and a supranational Europe, or even entire humanity, becomes the object to which they are attached. The subjective sense of belonging corresponds to a communicative networking that can be designated as transcultural. In contrast with the two former types, the range of communicative networking is more extensive, being either European or (imagined) global in tendency. The communicative network reaches across a wide variety of countries and cultures.

If the communicative figuration of the diaspora is to be kept in view *as a whole*, the different patterns of networking need to be considered together. It is characteristic of the mediatized world of today's diasporas to want to maintain communication links with the country of origin while also communicationally networking within the country to which they have migrated and with other areas. The communication networks of individual migrants, or the types according to which these can be systematized, can therefore be treated as a comprehensive communicative figuration. This is what one needs to come to terms with if one seeks to describe the mediatized world of today's migrant communitizations.

In this way one gains access to the way in which the present mediatized worlds of the diaspora can be described as a whole. Quite apart from all differences between modes of appropriation and contexts, it is possible to identify a moment which represents for migrants the existing, primary moulding forces of current media. *This is the prevailing immediacy of translocal communication by the media within the diaspora, an immediacy based upon the latest wave of mediatization.* Within the sphere of produced media communication, migrants can participate simultaneously in different communication spaces: watching satellite and Internet TV, downloading films, listening to Internet radio or reading online newspapers – all of these open up the possibility of participating, in parallel, in political and popular cultural discussions taking place in the country of origin, Germany and elsewhere in the world. And through the different forms of reciprocal media communication – whether based on the Internet or not – there is no problem at all in being networked-in to one's own family and circle of (migrant) friends, not only locally, but also translocally, comprehending all the different places in which members of the diaspora live, whether in the country of origin, in the land of migration, or in other countries. The different platforms of the social web also permit a comparatively simple way or organizing and representing such contacts. *We can talk here of moulding forces since this does not merely involve a possibility, but their simple existence always dominates the expectation of their use.* A clear example of this is how migrants living in today's mediatized world of the diaspora constantly are 'available to each other' through the use of (mobile) telephone or email. Supportive communication is *reciprocally institutionalized* through these media technologies. To the extent that we can characterize the diaspora as a specific mediatized world, we can also refer in general to 'mediatized migrants': for the way in which migrants live their lives in today's cultures of mediatization, technical communication media are of constitutive importance.

This brief outline of the results of our study should make quite clear where a consideration of the communicative figurations of mediatized worlds is going: it is not simply a matter of describing the appropriation of an individual medium, or a single communication network. Instead, a number of studies need to demonstrate the manner in which relations are set in motion through the communicative articulation of such mediatized worlds as a whole. This approach avoids the premature postulation of a media logic, and directs itself to the study of how mediatization is manifested in the various spheres of today's cultures of mediatization.

5

Communitization within Cultures of Mediatization

In the previous chapter a number of links between media cultures and communitization (*Vergemeinschaftung*) began to emerge. It is often said in the everyday world that the nation is not only a (media) culture, but also a community; there are cultures formed by social movements, such as the environmental movement, that also is a communitization of like-minded spirits. Everyday examples such as this clarify the kind of perspective adopted here: while the concept of (media) culture emphasizes the patterning of meaning, the concept of community – or, more properly, communitization as a process – points us towards the sense of belonging that someone feels to a particular figuration of people. These are related, but they are not the same thing: one feels a sense of belonging to a group of people 'distinguished' (sometimes deliberately and wilfully so) from others by particular 'characteristics'. These characteristics can be meaningfully interpreted as thickenings of particular cultural patterns, as well as the means of construction of communitization.

There has been a great deal of discussion in recent decades of the degree to which communitization has altered with the progressive mediatization of culture. For instance, there is Howard Rheingold's use of the term 'virtual communities' (1995), which is connected to our earlier discussion of cyberculture and Internet utopianism. Rheingold thinks that communities based upon direct communication are facing decline, and links this to his diagnosis of the loss of consciousness of things shared socially in common.

But what is lost, he argues, can be rescued by computer-mediated communication. This makes it possible to found new forms of communitization in cyberspace – his 'virtual communities'. These communitizations are based on a new, issue-orientated consciousness of community. At root, this is a matter of shared interests related to particular topics.

These ideas have prompted wide-ranging academic discussion (for an overview, see Deterding 2008). The chief line of argument against Rheingold concerns his utopianism, while the way in which he counters the 'real' with the 'virtual' has also been strongly criticized. Communitizations which form themselves through computer-mediated communication are, however, completely unbounded in regard to 'real' people and places, and, as Nancy Baym (2000) has shown, they cannot be described as a 'second reality' detached from everyday life.

More recently, Andreas Wittel has developed ideas related to 'network sociality', touched on in the previous chapter. These analyses are very instructive in regard to questions regarding networking processes and binding together through moulding media (technologies). More problematic, however, are his conclusions in respect of the relationship between network sociality and communitization. He considers that network sociality contrasts with community, that they are alternatives:

> The term 'network sociality' can be understood in contrast to community. Community entails stability, coherence, embeddedness, and belonging. It involves strong and long-lasting ties, proximity, and a common history or narrative of the collective. Network sociality stands counterposed to *Gemeinschaft*. . . . Network sociality consists of fleeting and transient, yet iterative social relations; of ephemeral but intense encounters. Narrative sociality often takes place in bureaucratic organizations. In network sociality the social bond at work is not bureaucratic but informational. . . . It is constructed on the grounds of communication and transport technology. (Wittel 2008: 157–8)

For Wittel, network sociality is the emphatic form of sociality in a 'network society' (Castells 2000). And in some sense here we are dealing once more with a scenario of decline, even if Wittel is strongly critical of Rheingold's arguments: according to Wittel, the stability, coherence and embeddedness of communities is giving way to the fluidity, transitoriness and informationality of the new network sociality.

There is no question that communitization is changing in today's cultures of mediatization, and Wittel's work can contribute a great deal to understanding particular aspects of this transformation. But we need to be clear that Wittel is talking about not the *transformation* of communitization, but its *loss*. In fact, although he criticizes Rheingold for replicating Tönnies' (2001) assumption that 'communities share a common geographic territory, a common history, a common value system' (Wittel 2008: 169), he does much the same thing. This sort of definition clearly takes us straight back to ideas about 'traditional' forms of communitization. Today we are aware that communitizations can be 'post-traditional', in the sense that affiliation 'is in principle *open* since this community is only an idea, something imagined' (Hitzler 1998: 86, emphasis in original). We also know that these communitizations are, in principle at least, scattered across very different territories. Membership of these scattered communities is gained not by traditional (local) allegiances, but instead by an individual choice which is in some respect independent of any particular geographical or social location. The experience of communitization thus becomes highly 'situated': whether occurring at particular music events or parties, or the kind of 'networking events' arranged in London's 'New Economy', as described by Wittel. It is therefore a matter not of the loss of communitization, but of its transformation in today's cultures of mediatization into something which is more translocal, post-traditional and situative.

If we are seeking some insight into these changes, how should we understand communitization? We can make use here of a very classical source which is sufficiently general to be applicable to contemporary changes. Max Weber defined the term in his 'Basic Sociological Concepts' as follows:

A social relationship will be called a 'communitization' if and to the extent that the orientation of social action rests – in the individual instance, or on average, or as a pure type – upon a subjectively *felt* (affectual or traditional) *mutual sense of belonging* among those involved. . . . It is only when their behaviour is in some way mutually *oriented* because of this feeling that a social relation is formed among them, a relation between each of them and the external world is insufficient; and it is only when this social relationship is registered as such that a 'community' can be said to have formed. (Weber 2013: §9, 22 §9.4, emphasis in original)

Here again we have the idea presented above, that communitization – insofar as this social relationship endures – involves patterned forms of reciprocal orientation, and hence relates to (media) culture.

Weber's definition is important as a point of departure in this chapter chiefly because it avoids two problems. Firstly, it does not assume a particular territorial foundation for community, but locates communitization in the character of a social relation. Communitizations can therefore be local, but can just as well be widely scattered. Weber's examples included the local domestic community; translocal, scattered communities of Christian brothers; *as well as* the territorial communitization of the nation. This potential translocality of communitization is not only of importance for questions of mediation (and hence mediatization) of communitization. It is also a concept susceptible to different scales: communitization can be 'small-scale' or 'large-scale', but in all cases it runs back to a specific social relationship involving a sense of belonging.

Secondly, Weber's definition lays emphasis upon the manner in which this sense of belonging is 'felt', something he does not simply associate with traditional forms. He thus draws attention to the fact that we also need to consider forms of communitization that are *non*-traditional, but which nonetheless involve a strong sense of belonging. In this respect, Weber's use of *Vergemeinschaftung* and *Vergesellschaftung* – communitization as felt belonging as against sociation as the rational pooling of interests – designates social figurational relationships that are neither opposed nor exclusive. The purposively rational sociation involved in office work can engender a sense of community among those working there – or not. Here we can already detect resonances of what Ronald Hitzler named 'post-traditional communitizations'. Zygmunt Bauman has called these 'aesthetic communities', and described their paradox of communitization as follows: '[S]ince it would betray or refute the freedom of its members were it to claim non-negotiable credentials, it has to take its entrances and exists wide open. But were it to advertise the resulting lack of binding power, it would fail to perform the reassuring role which for the faithful was their prime motive in joining in' (Bauman 2001: 65). This outlines the main issue to be discussed in this chapter: the question of the extent to which the emergence and transformation of contemporary forms of communitization are linked to the advance of mediatization of culture, at the (provisional) end of which process we find today's media cultures with their mediatized worlds.

Locality and Translocality

The contrast of locality to translocality made above involves two particular issues. The first relates to a specific feature of communication: that, as soon as it is media-mediated, it creates translocal connectivity. The second involves the character of media cultures, which, assuming this translocality of media communication, are themselves conceived to be translocal. The contrast of locality to translocality is, however, also relevant to the idea of communitization. *Local communitization* is based upon direct communication; it can be experienced 'directly', since we 'experience' all social relations through all our senses in terms of immediate communication. The community of a household is an example of this.

This involves a very particular concept of locality as 'being located', although we need to separate this from any naturalistic ideas (Massey 1994: 39). We can say that *a locality is a place of separated spaces, understood in relation to material or physical aspects and defined socio-culturally*. This place is controlled by people as it is constituted in their everyday practice, in which they make use of the resources made socially available to them. The meaning of a locality is articulated culturally and discursively, which means that it cannot be deduced from its materiality. The meaning of localities is likewise constructed through media, since they are themselves media sites (Hartmann 2009). Of course, the meanings of individual localities are also manifested by the particularities which people create or select. The extent of a locality – its cultural boundary – varies contextually. It makes sense therefore to treat a domestic environment, a procession or part of a town as a locality; but not of course a state, or a federation of states (since these are more to do with territory than with locality). In this sense, therefore, the concept of the local comprises *the networking space of localities that make up the everyday world of a person living in a particular cultural context. Local communitizations* are thereby characterized by the fact that they are local, hence can be experienced through direct communication, as noted above.

Translocal communitization is different, since it is not exclusively based upon and experienced as direct communication. This transcends any one place, and presupposes the existence of translocal communication. Translocal communitizations can be 'imagined' to different degrees, and we can here introduce Benedict Anderson's (1983) striking phrase 'imagined communities'. Curiously, discussion of this idea has focused almost exclusively on Anderson's initial object of analysis, the nation as imagined community. But his own understanding of the term is wider than that:

> In fact, all communities larger than primordial villages of face-to-face contact (and perhaps even these) are imagined. Communities are to be distinguished, not by their falsity/genuineness, but by the style in which they are imagined. ... The nation is imagined as *limited* because even the largest of them, encompassing perhaps a billion of living human beings, has finite, if elastic boundaries, beyond which lie other nations. (Anderson 1983: 6–7, emphasis in original)

This quote clearly shows that progressive mediatization lies at the core of the emergence and transformation of translocal communitization. This is shown by many studies. Anderson himself demonstrates that the emergence of the nation as a communitized entity was owed in part to the establishment of classical mass media and the formation of a national media culture: '[T] he novel and the newspaper . . . provided the technical means for "pre-presenting" the kind of imagined community that is the nation' (Anderson 1983: 25). This idea has been developed by John B. Thompson in his study *The Media and Modernity*, a work that we have referred to several times already. Thompson is, however, interested more in the emergence of the modern state than in the associated articulation of a national communitization. As we have also seen, Friedrich Tenbruck (1972) placed this in a historical framework using a range of societal types. But the importance of media communication is also emphasized for quite different kinds of translocal communitization, for example the diaspora (Dayan 1999). *Translocal communitization is therefore at least in part media-mediated communitization.*

The sociologist of religion and of knowledge Hubert Knoblauch (2008) has typified the differences arising between local and translocal communitization, arguing that the former should be treated as communities based upon knowledge, while the latter are communities based upon communication.

The reason for treating local communitization as involving *knowledge communities* – at least historically, as Tenbruck has done (1972: 59) – is that those partaking in enduring and strongly homogeneous communitization share a great deal of their knowledge in common. Because those affiliated with such communitizations are in continuous and direct contact with each other, much of their knowledge is 'unspoken' (Knoblauch 2008: 84), articulated especially in common activity. In a local knowledge community 'one knows where one is' and possesses knowledge that is not the subject of further communication. Such communities historically precede forms of translocal communitization.

The advance of mediatization also reveals a process of decontextualization and anonymization of communitization. Knoblauch associates the former with the fact, already discussed, that media-mediated interaction is related to the spatially and temporally extended availability of communication, replacing the co-present context with the separate contexts of communication. This is the multiplication of 'mediatized contexts' of communication (Knoblauch 2008: 82). If this media-mediated communication takes the form of the produced communication of mass media, we are additionally confronted with a process of anonymization. This is apparent in the way that interaction is no longer with particular others, but instead with a potential number of others (from the viewpoint of the communicator). This can be seen in the context of another aspect of cultural change, which manifests itself partly in the increasing differentiation of culture. Accordingly, one can no longer assume the existence of a shared knowledge. Moreover, in translocal communication what was hitherto implicit has now to be made explicit because of the limitations of means of communication. Translocal communitizations can therefore be characterized as *communication communities* that have developed during the most recent surges of mediatization. According to Knoblauch, what is decisive here is that the felt sense of belonging arising through communitization manifests itself in structured social relations:

> We can first talk of *communication communities* when these commonalities of communication and their objectification are also translated into social structures: whereas with TV, for example, only very weak 'public' social structures are formed (leaving aside groups like those of 'Corrie Fans', who actively construct their community), interactive media facilitate the creation of social structures: actors who reciprocally create networks dedicated to common issues (job search, homosexuality, phobias related to dentists) or forms (games, betting, auctions) without any doubt do constitute communication communities. . . . *Belonging to a community is for the most part effected through ongoing and parallel communication – overwhelmingly through communication, and not through tradition and knowledge.* (Knoblauch 2008: 2008, my emphasis)

Knoblauch does not claim that his account is empirical; it is, rather, a conceptual elaboration developed from a phenomenological approach. It is intended to form the basis for further

105

empirical study, whether historical or contemporary. It could also be said that the concepts of local knowledge community and of translocal communication community are ideal types of communitization, there being a number of transitional and hybrid forms lying between them. In this way the concepts are at the extremes of a continuum, at one end the purely local communitization of shared knowledge, at the other purely media-mediated translocal communities founded upon communication.

This conceptual work is of great help in our systematization of a descriptive panorama of (trans)local communitization. One should, however, exercise caution in seeking to force it into the form of a simple narrative of transition, to the effect that progressively the mediatization of translocal communitizations will gradually replace the local. This kind of approach would end up in the same kind of reductionism for which we have already criticized Medium Theory. Above all, one would in this way deny the possibility that in today's media cultures there is in fact a reciprocity between local and translocal communitizations.

Local communitization remains of central importance, even for the people of today's cultures of mediatization. As has been repeatedly emphasized, people, as always, live in particular places, and local communitization in these sites is a central element of the sense of belonging in our lives. Here again we can cite some of the forms of communitization that Max Weber noted (2009: 22), such as the 'erotic relationship' or the 'family'. Other examples are the communitization of a village or of a part of a town, although here there are of course also elements of separation and differentiation. In a village, for instance, while there is a distinction between membership of the voluntary fire brigade and of the sports club, one does not have to belong to both if one is to see oneself as part of the village community.

Local communitizations have not vanished with the development of mediatization. In regard to the change of today's media culture, something else seems to be going on. So, for example, local communitizations are mediatized in the sense that the articulation of separate feelings of belonging is also in part mediated by the media, and is facilitated by media. *Mediation by the media* is exemplified by the importance of the mobile phone in the life of modern couples (Linke 2011). *Media reference*, by contrast, has to take into account the degree to which the direct communication of family conversation is saturated with reconstructions of media contents, or with brief reference to them. This is particularly true when it is a matter of values and morality (Ulmer and Bergmann 1993; Keppler 1994; Hepp 1998). We cannot imagine today's communitizations as media-free zones. To the extent that they are communitizations of mediatized worlds in current media cultures, the processes of mediation by the media must always be borne in mind.

Translocal communitizations can be of the most diverse kind. This is shown in the examples advanced so far – starting with the nation, and moving on to issue-related communities of people with particular interests, orientations or problems. There is no such thing as *the* characteristic translocal form of communitization. What is specific to present-day cultures of mediatization is more the *variety of translocal communitization*, among which we can select those to which we feel we belong, in the same way that through our participation in specific processes of communication we become part of a process of communitization. It has to be remembered that these communitizations are trans*local*, that we remain connected to local life as a physical person. Correspondingly, despite all mediation by the media, translocal communitizations are manifested in local groups. Media communication forms in this way something like a horizon of meaning for communitization – an aspect to which I will return later.

In pursuing contextualization in this way it seems important to emphasize a central point in Knoblauch's argument: that the articulation of media-mediated, translocal communitizations presupposes the 'development of social structures' (Knoblauch 2008: 86). In the foregoing discussion it was stated that translocal communitizations involved both communicative *and* social networks. These could be of quite different kinds, since different media have different moulding forces. Moreover, these communication networks develop transmedially to a not inconsiderable extent. The communication network of a social scene – or, perhaps more exactly, the communicative figuration of a social scene – can be described in terms of diverse media such as fanzines, digital music, email, the social web, and so forth (see Hitzler and Niederbacher 2010: 30). The investigation of translocal communitization by media and communications specialists has to involve the empirical specification of individual communication figurations of today's cultures of mediatization.

Territorialization and Deterritorialization

The issue of territorialization and deterritorialization has already arisen several times in connection with translocal communitization, but also in connection with the discussion of the globalization of media communication. If we want to understand the translocal communitization of today's media communication, a rather more searching approach is in order. First of all we need to clarify the concepts of territorialization and deterritorialization.

Territorialization can be defined as the process in which an identifiable territory (a 'country', a 'region', a 'continent') is constructed as a physically anchored point of reference for a particular (media) culture, or as a form of communitization related to it. Perhaps the most widespread process of this kind is the articulation of national culture as the reference point for communitization: to be 'German' both culturally and communally, in both cases relating to the territory of 'Germany'.

Deterritorialization is, by contrast, the 'loosening' of this apparently 'natural' relationship between culture, communitization and territoriality. In respect of communitization, we need to distinguish two forms of deterritorialization: (i) the physical and (ii) the communicative.

Physical deterritorialization is addressed by globalization studies dealing with people's increasing global mobility (Pries 2001; Urry 2007; Favell 2008). A very large number of people travel and migrate in times of globalization, and the world as a whole is today more mobile than it has been in centuries past.

Communicative deterritorialization is related to the increas-

108

ing mediatization and globalization of media communication. Ever more media contents are available across diverse territories: TV formats such as soaps and quiz shows, together with films and music (videos) aimed at a transnational public (Hall 1997). Through this, media culture becomes at least in part deterritorialized. Material in the domains of youth and popular culture, which in a globalized age are communicated through media, is only to a small degree related to a particular territory.

Physical and communicative deterritorialization cannot, of course, be opposed to each other. They are, rather, interwoven at different levels. If one takes migrant communitizations or diasporas as an example of physical deterritorialization, it is plain that this is only because they are 'the exemplary communities of the transnational moment' (Tölölyan 1991: 3), since their members share a common cultural representation. And these shared common cultural representations, for instance the Bollywood films of the India diaspora, or the transnational Indian TV company ZeeTV (Thussu 1998), are ultimately mediated, based upon a communicative connectivity. Nonetheless, it is heuristically important to distinguish clearly between physical and communicative deterritorialization. There are three reasons for this in particular:

- *Speed*: communicative deterritorialization seems to happen much faster than the physical form. In the age of a global communicative infrastructure, media flows can be 'moved' much more quickly across different territories than can goods and people.
- *Volatility*: communicative deterritorialization seems to be much more 'volatile' than physical deterritorialization. If migration is taken as a leading example of the latter, then this process is very obvious in the local neighbourhood – a person is singled out as being 'foreign' by virtue of his or her everyday practices. This might also be the reason why classical sociologists took such a great interest in the social type of the 'stranger'. By contrast, many aspects of communicative deterritorialization are hard to identify, with, for example, 'nationalized' versions of transculturally distributed soap operas or quiz shows being

appropriated as 'national' TV, while the 'format' itself is deterritorialized (Moran 2009).

- *Reach*: apparently in contradiction with this is the issue of reach, in which communicative deterritorialization pervades mediatized worlds. This is much greater than with physical deterritorialization. While in many regions of the world physical mobility is less than one would think (Morley 2000: 86–104), media products of the most diverse kind are nonetheless available. Because of its speed and volatility, communicative deterritorialization extensively pervades mediatized worlds.

Here it will be useful to take up once more remarks made earlier regarding ideas of national culture and national communitization. If different localities are intensively linked to each other through media on a national and territorial level, then people can be linked through a communicative process which is aimed at the construction of an 'imagined community' (Anderson 1983) or a 'home territory' (Morley 2000). This highlights the extent to which questions of territoriality depend upon the construction of translocal national communities. This is especially evident in the history of TV: during the 1950s this was marketed as a 'window on the world', to use the contemporary advertising slogan. Advertising of this kind was of course aimed at local appropriation, in that TV had to find its place in domestic life (or in the village pub). From the perspective of communitization this was, however, a phase of nationalization, since the horizon of initial TV representations had a national-territorial foundation: the first important TV events were national festivals, national football games or national serials, and the broadcasting boundaries were likewise national. As print media and radio had done before, TV assisted in the articulation of an 'imagined community' of the nation.

Taking account of the above discussion of communitization, it is now possible to move beyond the idea that national mass media have to be dealt with as such, their translocal communicative thickenings being in this sense territorialized, national frontiers being then conceived as the primary boundaries of a variety of communicative networks and flows. In national media cultures there is also a communicative construction of a national community. This can be called *territorial translocal communitization*, which also corresponds to the thickenings of media culture. With the progressive mediatization and globalization of media communication, other media cultural thickenings and communitizations have gained in relevance: these are *deterritorial translocal communitizations*, which in turn correspond to analogous media cultural thickenings. This means that territoriality is *not* constitutive for the boundary of these cultural thickenings and communitizations.

If we take an overview, today a variety of territorial and deterritorialized translocal communitizations exist alongside each other, together with their corresponding cultural thickenings (see Figure 5.1). On the one hand there are more territorially focused thickenings of communicative connectivity, and for this reason it makes sense to talk of media-mediated 'regional' or 'national' translocal communitizations, together with their corresponding media cultures. On the other hand there are also communicative thickenings beyond these territorial boundaries, networks which open up a space for deterritorialized translocal communitizations with their corresponding media cultures.

Heuristically, there are at least four kinds of deterritorialized communitization that we need to distinguish: by ethnicity, theme, politics and religion. As regards ethnicity, there are an increasing number of communicative networks among diasporas. At the thematic level there is an increase of deterritorialized popular-cultural communitizations, those of a youth culture or a social scene, for example. At the political level, deterritorialized social movements are gaining in importance, for example that associated with the critique of globalization or the Occupy movement. Finally, religious communitizations represent a very old form of deterritorialized communities that have recently become of greater importance.

If this overview is to be extended, we need to emphasize that the analytically diverse forms of translocal communitization can blend into each other, or are contained within each other. For example, the migrant communitizations of the diaspora are quite capable of representing a characteristic popular culture. There is also a fluid

111

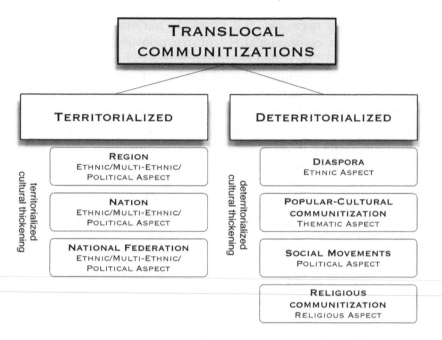

Figure 5.1 Translocal communitizations

transition between diasporas and the political communitization of social movements, if migrants become involved in the critique of globalization, or in the human rights movement, on the basis of their experience as migrants. Additionally, regional, national or supranational communitizations do not exclude each other. Alternatively, we can imagine processes in which deterritorialized communitizations and their corresponding media cultures are territorialized in communication processes: a once deterritorialized popular culture can become, for instance, a regional popular culture.

The overview given above must not be treated as a static representation. It needs constant development and revision on the basis of ongoing research into the changes in cultures of mediatization and their communitizations. However, while this overview is provisional, it does offer some understanding of the processes of translocal communitization in today's media cultures, and it should be read in this light.

Deterritorialized Communitizations

We now turn to examine deterritorialized translocal communitizations more closely. This has become especially relevant on account of recent surges in mediatization and globalization. Summarizing the foregoing, we can say that deterritorialized communitizations are translocal forms of communitization for whose communicative articulation territoriality is not constitutive. However different popular-cultural communitizations, diasporas, social movements or religious communitizations might be individually, analytically they fall into one of the following three categories:

- *Networks of local groups*: these deterritorialized communitizations are basically articulated in local groups whose members stand in direct communication with each other and are locally rooted. These different groups join themselves into an over-arching translocal social network.
- *Translocal horizon of meaning*: within these networks of deterritorialized communitizations there is a translocal horizon of meaning: that is, a common meaning orientation founding this communitization as such. This horizon of meaning is maintained through processes of media-mediated communication, hence through diverse mediatized communications networks which function transmedially through reciprocal communication (for example, chatrooms within social networks), and also through produced media communication (for example, the fanzines of a deterritorialized communitization).
- *Deterritorialized extension*: As suggested by the concept of deterritorialized communitization, the articulation of these translocal communitization networks does *not constitutively* depend upon a specific territory. But this does not mean that within these deterritorialized communitizations nationalization, or any other territorial connection, plays no role. In such networks it is possible to detect both national and regional thickenings. Nonetheless, deterritorialized communitizations are not shaped by such territorial thickenings.

113

Following on from these points, it becomes clear that if we are to appreciate change in communitization in today's cultures of mediatization, we need to direct our attention to the specifics of the communicative mediation of communitization. This concerns the communicative networks underlying these communitizations. Quite how they should be characterized is a matter of individual detail, and this has to be determined through empirical study of each particular case, the investigative context being also taken fully into account. Nonetheless, we still need to keep in view the individual elements of the four deterritorialized communitizations that are here distinguished heuristically.

I have referred above more than once to our own research on the mediatization of communicative networking within diasporas (Hepp et al. 2012). Hence I can summarize here, and provide some further contextualization for what has been argued so far. It is useful to talk of *ethnic aspects of deterritorialized communitization*, so long as one does not understand 'ethnic' as an essentializing concept. Stuart Hall (1992) rightly noted that ethnicity is a discursive construction, in which cultural properties such as language, custom and tradition are projected on to a 'community'. Likewise for the diaspora, we encounter constructions of ethnicity for which territoriality is not constitutive. It can be argued here that the gain in importance of this form of deterritorialized communitization with migration is founded upon both physical and communicative deterritorialization: the diaspora is spatially dispersed, but has available to it the possibility of creating and maintaining the most diverse communication networks among spatially scattered groups. Naturally this means that migration is not the same thing as the formation of a diaspora: the latter are not temporary, but rather imagined communitizations constituted by *enduring* translocal networks of relationship and communication (Clifford 1994: 311).

Of course, diaspora communities are historically a very 'ancient' phenomenon, the Jewish diaspora being a prominent example (cf. Cohen 2008). This case itself demonstrates how important media are for the maintenance of such communities, in this case the medium being religious texts. The progressive mediatization and globalization of media communication has gone beyond such religious traditions and prompted diverse rearticulations of diaspora communities (Bailey et al. 2007). Maintenance of the present diversity of diaspora communities and their identities would today be inconceivable without the possibility of permanently deploying, beyond the territorial frontiers of national states, communication networks based in particular upon satellite and Internet technology. Our finding here is supported by a number of other studies of diaspora connectivity (for example, Naficy 1993; Dayan 1999; Bromley 2000; Gillespie 2000; Silverstone and Georgiou 2005; Georgiou 2006). Empirical studies have detailed the appropriation of media by diaspora communities such as the Punjabi community in Britain (Gillespie 1995), the Trinidadian diaspora in the English-speaking world (Miller and Slater 2000) or the Turkish diaspora in Europe (Aksoy and Robbins 2000; Robins and Aksoy 2006, however avoiding the concept of communitization). Newer studies make clear that such communication networks involve the most diverse media, and that the arrival of the Internet and the mobile phone has led to this communication becoming more strongly synchronized (see Madianou and Miller 2011; Hepp at al. 2012).

Thematic aspects of deterritorialized communitization can be seen in popular-cultural communitizations. Since these are for the most part commercial in nature, membership is determined more by choice than by tradition. This is true for various social scenes, as well as for youth, fan and leisure cultures; and also for 'brand communities' created by companies around particular brands.

The way in which these thematically organized popular-cultural communitizations have been approached has varied. Zygmunt Bauman (2001) has used the term 'aesthetic communities', as we have already seen. The French sociologist Michel Maffesoli has used the concept 'neo-tribes' organized according to the fulfilment of particular functions or aims, but which have a thematic core of emotional communitization (Maffesoli 1996: 9f., 97; Keller 2008). This brings us to the discussion of 'post-traditional communitization' (Hitzler 2008a). This idea – not dissimilar to that of Maffesoli – seeks to express the fact that in contexts of progressive individualization different forms of commercialized recommunitization can be detected. There are various social scenes relating to leisure and consumption centred upon an organizing elite (which might have an interest in profits), and which offer the individual a temporary social involvement. The communitization of this kind of collective is post-traditional in the sense that affiliation is a matter not of tradition, but rather of individual participation, a temporary emotional attachment. Attachment to such a communitization in no respect involves a total commitment of the person concerned, and the attached are not simply unquestioningly accepted and socialized. The detailed studies by Hitzler and his colleagues of social scenes as a form of post-traditional communitization make clear how different communication networks overlap and interlock in the articulation of these scenes (see Hitzler and Niederbacher 2010). Among the elements involved are not only the communication networks of the organization's elite and local groups, but also the various forms of produced media used in the social scene (magazines and websites, music, etc.) through which much of the thematic content of the social scene is communicated.

Besides ethnic and commercial aspects we can also identify *political aspects of deterritorialized communitization*. It is obvious that use of the term 'political' in this connection relates less to political activity in state institutions than to what Ulrich Beck (1996) has called 'subpolitics'. Here we can locate a form of deterritorialized communitization, in the shape of social movements. The usual definition of social movements identifies them as networks of groups and organizations that seek to bring about, prevent or reverse social change through protest (Rucht 1994: 22f.). Nowadays, these movements start with everyday identity politics (Woodward 1997: 24). Political change – according to the credo of new social movements (Klein 2000) – occurs especially through changes of everyday human behaviour. This makes clear the way that these groups are concerned with relevant imagined communitizations for the articulation of identity, the translocal extension of these communitizations also being constituted through media. Consequently not only are the communicative networks of (alternative) media important for the constitution of new social movements (Atton 2002, 2004; Couldry and Curran 2003; Bailey et al. 2008), but also these movements develop their actual influence – their identity politics – through commercial media representations.

The importance of media to social movements is demonstrated by the political communitization of globalization critics (Hepp and Vogelgesang 2005). Initially this relates back to politically engaged local groups that have developed in different parts of the world. The emergent network of groups of globalization critics is not only aimed at the achievement of political objectives in the usual sense of the term, such, as for example, restricting the influence or profit-making prospects of deterritorialized (media) companies. In addition, it is a question of both intervention-orientated identity politics and the articulation of identity related to local communitizations. Hitzler (2002) argues that the anti-globalization movement can be treated as a 'moving social scene' (see also Bemerburg and Niederbacher 2007) whose aim as a social movement is clearly directed against the negative aspects of globalization, but which has at the same time found a connection with other commercialized forms of communitization. This means that the anti-globalization movement constitutes itself through communicatively networked local groups and organizes its events or demonstrations both for the sake of politics and for simply having fun, which events are then in turn intended to be diffused in produced form through the usual mass media or the Internet (cf. Barker 2002: 182f.; Jong et al. 2005: 1). It is the associated event-based representation of the anti-globalization movement in different media that moves it forward as a deterritorialized imag-ined community, just as representation in the media is central to its politics. Manuel Castells ascribes a great deal of transformational potential to such deterritorialized political communitizations, insofar as they can produce 'project identities'. These project identities offer a new power of identity by initiating social change through 'aiming at the transformation of society as a whole, in continuity with the values of communal resistance to dominant interests enacted by global flows of capital, power, and informa-tion' (Castells 1997: 357).

117

The fourth aspect of deterritorialized communitization is that of religion. It is not easy to identify clearly the boundaries of the concept of *religious communitization*. Present-day discussion understands religion to be a system of meaning or signification (including related teaching, confession and institution) that has a transcendental claim to symbolic interpretation going beyond the everyday. Religion lends everyday life a 'deeper' meaning which is manifested in daily religious practice, and is indicative of a related communitization. On this basis we can understand 'religion' in its various shades as a general orientation to a corresponding transcendent system of meaning.

Although there is nothing new in drawing attention to the deterritorialized nature of religion as a whole, we can say that the development of mediatization and globalization has also brought about a change in religious communitization. Historically, a great deal of effort went into maintaining communication among scattered groups through, for instance, the use of peripatetic preachers (Winter 1996). Globalization and mediatization, by contrast, facilitate a more intensive development of communication networks among religious communities. This is very plain in the case of traditional organizations such as the Roman Catholic Church, which, by introducing a World Youth Day in 1986, created an event which conveyed to young believers the sense of a deterritorialized communitization of Catholics, but which also created something to be more widely reported both within the Church and in the wider media, networking religious communities on a lasting basis. World Youth Day is in this respect a 'hybrid religious media event', combining the traditional pattern of religious festivities with that of a popular media event (for the following see Hepp and Krönert 2010). Mediatization is evident here at several levels: in organizing World Youth Day, the Catholic Church aims at raising its media profile, and thus organizes the large sacred events in the form of a 'TV church service' exemplifying 'media belief' so as to suit the produced communication of the mass media. Street celebrations not directly organized by the Church are also reported on, together with all other popular events. To integrate all this, the Pope plays the role of 'media celebrity' (for Protestantism see also Lundby

118

2006). Participation in World Youth Day through mobile phones, digital cameras, video screens and other communicative possibilities ensures that the event is comprehensively mediatized. All of this is ultimately aimed at creating a 'religious brand' for the Catholic Church as a deterritorialized, mediatized religious community.

In regard to media cultures, there are two relevant spheres concerning religious communitization: the popular-religious spiritual sphere and fundamentalist movements. The concept of spirituality involves a form of religiosity in which personal experience plays a central part in religious orientation. These movements initially distanced themselves from traditional forms of organized religion and their dogmatic teaching (see Knoblauch 2009). Within religious communities, spiritual movements are nothing new, but they have in the past few years developed very rapidly. This applies both to spiritual movements within Christianity (for example, Charismatics and Pentecostalists) and to the Sufi movement within Islam. In addition there are (transcultural) spiritual movements which until the late 1990s were generally characterized as New Age movements, but which are, rather, an alternative form of religion that originated in the late 1960s (Knoblauch 1989). As Knoblauch established, a general orientation to spiritual experience gave rise to movements which could be most accurately described as transcultural hybrids. They not only revived elements of archaic 'Western religions' (for instance, Celtic or Germanic rituals); they also integrated and modernized 'Eastern elements' such as techniques of meditation and combined them with occultism, magic and esotericism, and even spiritual elements of Catholicism. Spiritual movements composed of the 'new religious', or believers in 'Eastern mysticism', had no specific teachers or traditional church-based organization. Instead, they were networks of persons and local groups with a specific spiritual orientation, able to keep in touch with each other thanks to various forms of media communication through the Internet (related websites, for instance), through traditional mass media (esoteric publications, for example) or through related events. As such they mark a general trend in the change of religion within the context of mediatization (Hoover 2006).

Religious events are themselves to be understood as mediatized phenomena, exemplified by the social events organized around Marian apparitions. Even if the dramaturgy of these events is organized more around a (traditional) liturgy than a show, it remains a mediatized liturgy in which the religious apparition is focused on audio and video recording to document the event (Knoblauch 2009: 224–5). Through this a mediatized event takes place which, like World Youth Day, is hybrid in nature. As defined by Knoblauch, a 'popular religion' is marked out by the way that 'a religion adapts itself to the new form of popular culture' (2009: 198).

Although the spiritual movements outlined have seldom been officially recognized, despite their rapid growth, it is fundamentalist movements of this form of deterritorialized religious communitizations that have become objects of public criticism. One variant is Islamic fundamentalism, which in its present form is also a reaction to globalization. Media reporting freely treats such fundamentalist movements as prototypically religious, although academic studies have repeatedly emphasized that this is only *one* form of a deterritorialized religious communitization. In regard to fundamentalist movements we can here refer once more to Castells' argument that they are, at least in part, a reaction to problems of globalization. Included here are religious fundamentalist movements that have formed entirely in 'the West'. Following Castells, we can define a deterritorialized religious communitization as fundamentalist if those affiliated to it treat a norm derived from a divine decree as an ultimate authority, and formative for any action (cf. Castells 1997: 12). Fundamentalism understood in this way stands in contrast to spiritual movements by virtue of the centrality of 'dogma' and (re)organized religious teaching – even if they share revivalist tendencies.

Placing differences on one side, both popular religious spiritual and fundamentalist movements have in common a mediatized form of religious belonging which is informed no longer by tradition, but rather by a positioning of the mediatized construction of tradition (cf. Schipper 2005). The members of today's religious communities are on a common footing with members of any other contemporary media culture in articulating their religious sense of belonging within the framework of a mediatized 'common culture' (Hoover 2006: 289).

The Mediatized Subjective Horizons of Communitization

I hope to have shown that the specific nature of communitization in today's media cultures does not lie in its increasing 'virtualization'. It is more appropriate to think in terms of an increasing mediatization of communitization. In addition to being a 'translocal phenomenon', increasing mediatization and globalization render communitization 'imagined', relying on communication networks and communicative figurations beyond exclusively territorial references. The increasing translocal reach of communication processes has raised the profile of deterritorialized communitizations, for which territoriality is not a constitutive category.

The distinction made above between ethnic, thematic, religious and political aspects of such deterritorialized communitizations is a heuristic one, and there are many compounds of these different elements. This is most plain in the popular-cultural elements of spiritual religious communitizations. Another example is the open-source movement, which is characterized by thematic as well as political aspects of communitization (Tepe and Hepp 2007): the thematic orientation to software development is linked to the (sub) political aspiration that code should be freely available.

These hybrid forms lend emphasis to the *increasing complexity of mediatized communitization*. Not only does this complexity involve the existence of many hybrid forms, but from a *subjective perspective* the different aspects of communitization are overlaid upon one another: membership of one social movement does not necessarily exclude membership of a popular-cultural communitization. The same is true for membership of a diaspora or of a religious communitization. Likewise membership of both territorial and deterritorialized communitizations is from a subjective standpoint quite probably more normal than not: one sees oneself *both* as British and as part of the globalized movement opposed to atomic power, for example. We need to view mediatized communitizations not only from the perspective of communitization itself, but also from the subjective viewpoint of the individual.

To determine what the *subjective perspective of communitization* might look like, we can once again make use of Alfred Schütz and Thomas Luckmann's social phenomenology. They present the everyday world as something that is experienced unquestioningly. Action in the everyday world is treated initially as unproblematic. However, this lack of questioning is hedged around with uncertainties:

> One experiences that which is taken for granted as a kernel of determinate and straightforward content to which is cogiven a horizon which is indeterminate and consequently not given with the same straightforwardness. This horizon, however, is experienced at the same time as fundamentally determinable, as capable of explication. .... [W]hat is taken for granted has its explicatory horizons – horizons therefore of determinable indeterminacy. (Schütz and Luckmann 1973: 9)

We can relate these ideas to questions of translocal communitization: what is taken for granted and experienced as such involves not only communitization in a group based upon direct communication, but also elements of translocal communitizations founded upon reciprocal media communication – telephoning or exchanging mail with friends at other sites, for example. Extensive translocal horizons of meaning of communitization are 'determinable indeterminacies' insofar as they are based not on a direct or reciprocal experience of communication, but on 'ideas' or 'imaginations' which can form through the use of produced media communication.

If we consider this from a subjective perspective we can say that for each individual person there is a complex whole of meaning horizons for communitization in which that person is situated, with, of course, situational variation. This whole can be termed the *subjective horizon of communitization*. For the individual person this is initially a 'determinable indeterminacy', in that it forms an unproblematic frame of reference of communitization in the everyday world. Individual elements of the horizon of communitization – especially the horizon of meaning for translocal communitizations based upon media-mediated communication processes – can, however, become problematic as a result of different experiences. Here direct local and mediated translocal experience are related. To take an example: conflicts among local religious groups can place in question the translocal communitization of this religion if a particular local act is thought to be incompatible with what is regarded as specific to affective relationships in the communitization as a whole. We have seen how this happens in our study of World Youth Day as a media event: an engaged young Catholic turned his back on the Catholic community after the local priest barred him and his group from the parish rectory because their music was 'too loud'. The bonds established by the experience of a media event and the communitization thereby communicated are limited if not grounded in that local action and experience.

It can be said of today's cultures of mediatization that the subjective horizon of communitization is carried by diverse (media) communication networks. It is in this respect comprehensively mediatized. To begin with, this affects all elements of translocal communitization. As has been argued above, their horizons of meaning are established and maintained through media communication in all its forms – one could go as far as to say that a broadly translocally directed subjective horizon of communitization is only conceivable in a media culture. If the relationship between a couple is once more taken as an instance of local communitization, this becomes more plain. It can be shown that the relationship of a young couple, and their experience of communitization, is saturated by their common appropriation of media (cf. Linke 2011). Within the couple's relationship not only is a repertoire of media communication specific to the relationship under constant negotiation – that is, a repertoire of media used in common; the relationship of the couple is also organized on a daily basis through the continuing use of media. Of importance here are mobile phones and Internet-based media such as chatrooms. This is not simply a matter of co-ordinating their actions, but includes the organization of social events involving media, such as watching TV together or playing a computer game, both of which in turn have as their aim the communitization of the couple's relationship. Here we can talk of the mediatization of the couple relationship. This exemplifies the way in which local moments of subjective horizons of communitization in today's media cultures likewise need to be understood as mediatized.

Examples such as these bring us to questions of *communicative mobility*, which, it is thought, are increasingly characteristic of today's experience of the local. This expression is directed to an understanding of the relationship between media and increasing local mobility in today's media cultures. This relationship can take two forms. Firstly, the 'end-user' equipment of media communication itself has become increasingly mobile. Examples would be mobile phones, laptops, BlackBerrys, MP3 players, mobile digital TVs and DVD players, mobile game consoles and different forms of 'wearable computing'. Secondly, communicative mobility also means that stationary media are increasingly directed to people on the move. Raymond Williams' remarks on the 'mobile privatization' of modern European societies (2003: 19) show that these features of communicative mobility were already apparent with the TV as a produced medium of communication. The television created a more or less stable, central space of communication for people who shifted between different places – the home, the workplace. Other examples of the focus upon mobility of stationary media would be the CCTV cameras that watch over people in movement, or the use made of Internet cafés while travelling in maintaining relations of communication.

This definition of communicative mobility has to be seen in relation to another form of mobility: *local mobility*. This has a dual sense. On the one hand there is situational local mobility (the movements of one person during a day, or a week, or a month, while commuting to work, for example). Local mobility in this sense does not mean 'jetting across the world', or, at any rate, mostly not; it is, rather, a movement between defined places. This was the form of mobility that Williams had in mind when proposing the idea of mobile privatization. On the other hand we have something like a biographical local mobility (as part of the lifetime of a person, in the form of migration, for example). We consequently have to relate mediatized subjective horizons of communitization to questions of communicative mobility. Situational local mobility characterizes the everyday world of many people in today's cultures of mediatization (for an overview see Urry 2007). This can be a regular commute between home and work, but it can also assume more complex forms, such as finding oneself in different places of work while on foreign service. In all situations like this the appropriation of different media serves to maintain reciprocal media communication in a relational network, where even with peripatetic local mobility enduring relationships and elements of communitization that have importance are supported by media communication (Berg 2010). This is even more clear in the case of biographical local mobility, the most obvious example of which is migration and the associated communities of the diaspora. Their specifically translocal communitization can hardly be understood if one neglects questions of local mobility.

The subjective horizon of communitization is closely related to the *cultural identity* of a person. Identity is not something static, but is an ongoing process of identification (Hall 1992). This formulation has two aspects. Firstly, from the perspective of symbolic interactionism, identity arises in the interaction between an 'I' and 'society'. Secondly, Stuart Hall's articulation theory rejects the idea that there is a lasting 'ego' or 'subject' as the essential centre of a person. Each subject, at different times and in different contexts, adopts different identities. These identities cannot be unified into a context-free 'ego' which is the 'core of an identity'.

Rather than talk of identity as something fixed and complete, it makes more sense to think of identity as an ongoing process of articulation which presupposes a communicative, contextually situated demarcation with respect to a menu of possible identities. For cultural identity in today's cultures of mediatization, its connections to 'society' depend to a great extent upon the subjective horizon of communitization. The horizon of communitization of an individual person is to a very great degree manifested in that person's cultural identity. Or to put it another way: the identifications which make up the totality of a person's cultural identity in present cultures of mediatization are to a great extent identifications with particular local and translocal communitizations.

Insofar as this horizon of communitization is itself mediatized, we can here talk of *media identities* as a further characteristic of cultures of mediatization. This does not, however, mean that *all* of our present identity is mediated through media. Many of the experiences upon which the articulation of identity rests come from direct communication. Nonetheless, it can be argued that the *form of identity* characteristic of media cultures cannot be conceived without media communication. To take a fictional example: the cultural identity of a particular person in that person's simultaneous membership of and identification with a nation, the anti-globalization movement, Buddhism and the HipHop community expresses, indicates, that the horizon of meaning of all these communitizations is not only mediated by the media, but also mediatized. This is what is meant if we talk of media identities.

6

Studying Cultures of Mediatization

The previous chapters of this book dealt with the characteristics of media cultures as cultures of mediatization: as a consequence of their mediatization they are characterized by the moulding forces of the media, and their everyday life is transformed into the life in mediatized worlds. These worlds can in turn be characterized by quite particular communicative figurations, where the subjective horizon of communitization is for the most part conveyed medially. These are statements about media culture that need making, and they should encourage us to approach these aspects of media culture in a more differentiated empirical manner. The preceding chapters outline a conceptual framework with which we can approach media cultures, but a framework that has to be developed through empirical research. From that it follows that this book about cultures of mediatization rightly ends with the question: what do we need to look for, watch out for, in pursuing the investigation of media culture?

There is not enough space here to provide a comprehensive introduction to the empirical study of media culture. That would have to be another book, a book which, despite the number of existing introductions to the empirics of media and communication, remains unwritten. Something different can be done here: we can outline a methodological framework for empirical research into cultures of mediatization, and this is what the following seeks to do. As an outline, it will be organized in four phases: the development of theory; decentring; pattern analysis; and, finally, transcultural comparison.

Developing Theories

It has been repeatedly emphasized in the foregoing that media cultures are currently undergoing far-reaching changes. We cannot be sure that our established theoretical framework is adequate to an understanding of these changes and their consequences. Nor can we say with any certainty, faced with such continuing change, whether the categories and concepts that we already possess will be of lasting validity. For these reasons it is important to do a kind of research that is orientated to the (further) development of theories as well as to the seeking of new frameworks.

Here we can refer again to Sonia Livingstone's (2009) reflection on the increasing 'mediation of everything'. Her discussion of conceptions such as mediation and mediatization takes due account of the experience of deep-seated changes in the role that media communication plays in today's world. It is no longer a matter of treating media as independent institutions that have an impact upon other institutions. Instead, we need to take account of the fact that we live in worlds that are saturated with media communication – in cultures of mediatization, as has been argued throughout this book. Acknowledging this represents a challenge for the study of media and communication as hitherto practised as this practice has very much focused upon the analysis of institutions of mass communication.

To take the argument of Livingstone further: discussion of mediatization is really all about the development and revising of prospective concepts, categories and terms. These need in turn to be adequate for an understanding of the contemporary importance of media communication. Assuming that imperatives such as these are not merely rhetorical, but have a substantive foundation, we can ask: what does it mean to develop new theories?

One source which can help us respond to this is 'grounded theory'. This originated when a similar problem faced the discipline of sociology during the later 1960s. The American sociologists Barney Glaser and Anselm Strauss argued for materially grounded theoretical development in terms that will be familiar to those working in media and communication studies today.

They suggested that sociology was increasingly preoccupied with the use of existing theories, testing the principal theories of classical sociological thinkers 'in small ways' against new fields of objects, with the aim of modifying and reformulating these theories (Glaser and Strauss 1967: 10). However, such an approach precluded the development of new and original theories. It was assumed that eventually sociology would become a treasure trove of 'grand theories' which could then be applied to different fields, the theories themselves being open to only very limited development.

Glaser and Strauss argued, however, that 'the masters have not provided enough theories to cover all the areas of social life that sociologists have only begun to explore' (1967: 11). On top of this, many of the theories advanced by the classical thinkers were inadequate, since they lacked the methods needed to theoretically evaluate relevant data. Most importantly, however, it can be said that human relations faced an ongoing process of change, and that we confront today socio-cultural phenomena that classical theories could not have anticipated. Consequently, Glaser and Strauss called for a transition in the practice of sociological work: from research aimed at testing theories, to research aimed at the generation of new theories.

Their proposal was for the development of 'grounded theory', arguing that new theories could be developed directly from empirical work on particular spheres of phenomena. Theories could emerge from the comparative analysis of qualitative material – transcripts of interviews, observations, records of meetings, photographs, etc. – from which, step by step, first of all substantive conceptions could be roughed out, followed by the elaboration of more abstract categories. The latter would be the foundation for grounded theory. Such theory had a material basis because the form of its development was 'grounded' in a particular field of study.

Glaser and Strauss here distinguished two forms of theory that could be derived from such comparative analysis: substantive and formal theories:

By substantive theory, we mean that developed for a substantive, or empirical, area of sociological inquiry, such as patient care, race relations, professional education, delinquency, or research organizations. By formal theory, we mean that developed for a conceptual, or formal, area of sociological inquiry, such as stigma, deviant behavior, formal organization, socialization, status congruency, authority and power, reward systems, or social mobility. (1967: 32)

Both kinds of theory are related, since formal theory was derived from the comparative analysis of key categories identified from among a range of substantive theories. Hence various substantive theories regarding the constitution of a social scene, such as Black Metal, HipHop, live action role play, and so forth, made possible a formal theory of the creation of social scenes in general. This is exactly what the empirical studies of Ronald Hitzler and Arne Niederbacher (2010), which I have discussed above, have sought to do. Formal theories therefore integrate in turn very diverse substantive theories by examining the comparative formation of categories.

Glaser did, however, later (2007) note that grounded theory had devoted too much effort to the development of substantive theories. They had as it were rather lost sight of formal theory, which is important for successfully understanding a changing social reality through a general conceptual apparatus. Glaser has also since insisted that formal theories are *not* 'so-called "grand theory", general theory' (2007: 100). They remain 'grounded' by virtue of the linkages between substantive theories. The level of a formal theory's abstraction is related to the focus: this can involve a formal theory of particular social relationships, of particular institutions, or other contexts. In this book we therefore encounter many of the ideas already raised above concerning questions of scale – in this case, the scalability of formal theory.

This therefore involves, with substantive as well as formal theory, the type of substantively based theory identified in Chapter 3 (Type 2 in Table 3.1). And it can generally be said that the path proposed by Glaser and Strauss is only one of several possible paths for the development of new theories. Other procedures do exist for the development of theory in the fields of ethnography or heuristic social research (for the latter see Krotz 2005). There are also further research traditions orientated to substantively founded theoretical development, such as cultural studies; and these likewise involve theorization based on individual studies, and not on the evaluation of a 'grand theory' (Morley 1998). We have available to us a number of approaches to the development of theory, some of which include standardized or statistical data. Despite their differences, all these approaches meet on the one point: they seek to develop theories from empirical analysis which will permit us to grasp socio-cultural phenomena in an appropriate manner. This appropriateness can – and this is the main argument – be secured by the fact that the development of theory remains grounded in substantive material, whatever moves it seeks to make.

These remarks explain the following consideration: we can argue that the previous general metatheoretical consideration of the mediatization of culture (a Type 3 theory in Table 3.1) gives us a 'panorama' of media and communicative change which should be the starting point for an empirical investigation orientated to theory development. The existing metatheory of mediatization is not (yet) an 'answer', but instead a point of departure to pose the questions relevant to media culture: how are social relationships formed in today's cultures of mediatization? What is the nature of play in present mediatized worlds? How is politics articulated within contemporary media cultures? These and many other questions which, in Glaser and Strauss's conceptualization, aimed at the construction of formal theories need to be broken down so that they can be used to study particular grounded spheres of phenomena (particular couples, specific forms of mediatized games, a demarcated type of mediatized politics, and so on). It should not, however, be forgotten that such research is aimed at the development of formal theories. This reciprocity then provides a basis for the conduct of further empirical research into today's cultures of mediatization.

Therefore, setting the framework for a metatheory of mediatization and its reflection in a concept of media culture, as proposed in this book, does not render research orientated to theoretical development obsolete. It should quite certainly *not* involve the elaboration of a Grand Theory which then simply has to be 'applied' to the various contexts of the empirical world. Rather, these metatheoretical reflections are intended to provide access to our contemporary life, an access which makes it possible for us to pose particular research problems. By postulating a comprehensive mediatization of culture on the basis of the existing state of knowledge we can pose specific questions to individual spheres of phenomena of media culture. The aim is to facilitate a diverse, theoretically orientated approach to research which is much less reliant on a 'meta' level, and which ideally involves a number of formal theories.

Decentring

Throughout this book there has been an emphasis on the increasing mediatization of culture, but David Morley (2007, 2009) has recently cautioned that we should not unreflectingly exaggerate the centrality of media. Instead, he has put forward the notion of 'non-mediacentric media studies', describing this approach as follows:

> Clearly enough, in the present context, we have to move beyond media studies' historically rather exclusive focus on television so as to also address the contemporary significance of a broader range of communication technologies. However, I shall also argue that we need to 'decentre' the media, in our analytical framework, so as to better understand the ways in which media processes and everyday life are interwoven with each other. The problems we face will not be solved by contemporary proposals to 'modernize' media studies by reconceptualizing it as 'web studies' or the like, for this would simply be to put the internet at the centre of the equation, where television used to stand. Such a move would merely replicate a very old technologically determinist problematic in a new guise. The key issue here, to put it paradoxically, is how we can generate a non-mediacentric form of media studies, how to understand the variety of ways in which new and old media accommodate to each other and coexist in symbiotic

forms and also how to better grasp how we live with them as parts of our personal or household 'media ensemble'. (Morley 2007: 200)

Here Morley deals with arguments that have been discussed in this book, relating them to the study of media and communications. The changes in media communication with which we are presently confronted have great significance for the academic discipline that has sought to understand its phenomena. It *can no longer* be a discipline that focuses only on the produced media of newspaper, TV, radio and film; it needs to deal with the diversity of contemporary media-mediated forms of communication. The idea that it can concentrate upon selected individual media has become increasingly problematic: for example, the Internet is not one single thing but involves very different forms of media-mediated communication using *one* technical infrastructure, and its omnipresent accessibility has an impact on ever more areas of our everyday life. Media and communication studies must direct its attention more to what Morley calls 'media ensembles', what in the foregoing is described as a totality of mediatized worlds organized through communication networks and communicative figurations. In other words: this involves a transmedial approach to questions of (media) communication. At the same time, a trans-medial perspective of this kind should not be 'mediacentric', but must instead 'decentre the media' and contextualize it.

This idea of decentring brings us back to our discussion of Nick Couldry's conception of 'mediated centres'. This idea of a media-mediated centre helps us understand the centrifugal forces of media today. In many respects the idea of a 'mediated centre' represents the myth that the media – by which is meant the produced media communication of the mass media – offer privileged access to the heart of a media culture: 'the media' communicate what is thought 'most important' in such a culture (see Couldry 2006). While we might think this a myth, it is one that can be taken seriously and analysed in terms of 'media rituals', those varied rituals in which the people living in a media culture confirm the centrality of media and so construct a 'mediated centre'. Particular media events can be considered here: royal weddings, world championships, even the Catholic World Youth Day, which has already been discussed (Hepp and Couldry 2010). But the events can equally be the small rituals of everyday life: the hourly scanning of online newspapers during the day, switching the TV on for the evening news, or reading the daily paper in the morning, through all of which the centrality of media in present media cultures is habitualized and ritualized. If one adopts this perspective, then *decentring* means above all: analysing the process through which media, along a diversity of strands, are *constructed* as '*central*' within today's cultures of mediatization.

One problem in respect of questions of mediatization could possibly be that the conception of a 'mediated centre' remains linked to an older approach to the study of media and communication which is concerned with the classical mass media orientated to one specific broadcaster or publisher, rather than the media environment within which they function and which they shape. In media cultures, saturated as they are with technical media orientated to reciprocity in communication, the classical mass media lose their pre-eminence – so runs the argument. Correspondingly, the construction of a 'mediated' centre is weakened.

Uwe Hasebrink has therefore suggested that we shift our attention towards the use of various media by any one individual. It is less a matter of studying the appropriation of an individual medium, but instead one of the 'media repertoire' of a person or a group of persons as a totality of media (Hasebrink and Popp 2006; Hasebrink and Domeyer 2010). So according to this line of argument, if we want to find out about 'atomic energy', we not only talk to several people, but also use a variety of media – newspapers, TV, the web, and so on.

Couldry has taken up this issue. While he shares Hasebrink's perspective, he places the emphasis rather differently. As he states: 'Instead of interpersonal media becoming divorced from centrally produced media flows and offering an alternative social "centre" to that offered by the media, it is more likely that "social" media and centrally produced media become ever more closely linked' (Couldry 2009: 444–5). The so-called social media of Web 2.0 are increasingly combined with classical mass media and their digital complements. For instance, Wikipedia first became known through articles in (online) newspapers and periodicals; Facebook is used to advertise classical produced media contents; online discussions are referred to in TV broadcasts, and so forth. It can be argued therefore that Internet-based media do not *necessarily* displace the articulation of a 'mediated centre'. As Couldry suggests, 'Instead of collapsing, "the media" will become a site of struggle for competing forces: *market-based fragmentation* vs. *continued pressures of centralization* that draw on new media-related myths and rituals' (2009: 447, my emphasis).

Nonetheless, it remains important to extend the idea of media-centrism with regard to questions of mediatization. To some extent in today's cultures of mediatization we have an 'everyday media-centrism'. Here access to and the use of digital media are considered 'central'. One example would be what could be called 'mobile telephone centrism', relating to the moulding forces of the mobile phone. In present media cultures it is not only *expected* that one has a mobile phone; *because of* this one can be reached at any time or place, at least for a particular group of people. If someone goes against this, it is necessary to argue for such a position quite explicitly, since it is no longer 'the norm': owning and using a mobile phone count as 'central' for present personal communication. Here we can see how the 'small forms' of media-centrism work, in which discourses of produced media communication (advertising, for example) and discourses of reciprocal media communication (the discursive practice of a mobile phone) interlink.

Decentring therefore has two senses. Firstly it involves an analysis of processes through which, in today's cultures of mediatization, the ownership and use of particular media come to be regarded as communicatively central – in other words, important. Secondly it involves analysis of the processes through which the diverse forms of media communication are construed as the form of access to the primary resources of media culture. The two can be connected, but not necessarily.

Study of this must, however, contextualize 'the media', or, more exactly, media communication. As already shown in the discussion of mediatization, there is little point in dealing with 'the media' as if they had their own individual and inherent 'logic'. There are no such unitary phenomena in the domain of mediatization. Instead, we have to deal with different forms of technically mediated communication which are always placed in a specific context. Although there has been very stimulating discussion of the implications of this point among those working in media and communication studies (for example, Lull 1987; Morley and Silverstone 1991; Schröder 1994; Ang 1996), we need here to focus on something else: if we place 'media' in the context of a non-mediacentric conception of media and communication, then in some cases it can turn out that 'media' have less importance for particular aspects of today's everyday worlds than had been thought.

Analysing Patterns

Throughout this book emphasis has been placed on the importance of a focus upon cultural patterns in the conduct of empirical media research. We need now to clarify quite what we mean by 'pattern'. In so doing it is helpful to recall the idea that media culture is a thickening of classificatory systems and discursive formations, to which the articulation of meaning in everyday life is practically connected. If this is related to the contemporary discussion of a praxiological approach to cultural research (Reckwitz 2005: 96), it integrates all three established discourses in the tradition of social constructivism: mentalist (emphasizing the importance of classificatory systems), textual (emphasizing the relevance of discursive formations) and praxiological (emphasizing the importance of routine daily practices). The idea here is to keep in view the centrality of everyday practices in the articulation of culture, while at the same time allowing for the fact that cultures cannot be reduced to such daily practices. Culture is just as present in discursive formations and systems of classification, and we take this into account in our behaviour. In the majority of cases we do so quite unconsciously, without having any 'discursive consciousness' in the sense of Anthony Giddens (1984): we are not capable of describing in our own words the pattern of discourses within which we operate.

But we need to take account of the fact that such a differentiation is heuristic: for example, Actor-Network Theory shows that 'thinking' is based on (material) knowledge practices (Latour 2007). Discourse analysis has shown that discourses are produced through practices, and create a particular form of knowledge (Foucault 1994). Practices are also themselves conducted on the basis of sedimentized mental relevance structures, as social phenomenology has shown (Schütz 1967). Therefore, it is *generally* a question of defining cultural patterns and can be done in relation to very many features of media culture.

It can be argued that empirical media research into cultural patterns should be conducted in different ways, according to the given object of study and questions raised, while at the same time reflecting reciprocities. The use of the expression 'pattern' is rather misleading if this is thought to be something 'static'. We need to bear in mind that we are dealing with patterns in a process. Generally the term 'pattern' is intended to provide for the fact that in studying media culture we are not addressing ourselves to singular phenomena, but are seeking instead the *typical* forms in a particular cultural context on the basis of the analysis of different singular phenomena.

Hence cultures of mediatization are treated as thickenings of particular cultural patterns. And here another aspect of thickening is important. Many of the cultural patterns that are described are not exclusive to the analysed media culture. This is where the general hybridization of media culture manifests itself. The specific qualities of media culture as a territorial or deterritorial thickening are evident in the *total articulation* of particular reciprocities of various cultural patterns. The term 'thickening' here lends emphasis to the specificity of a media culture in the entirety of its pattern, as well as the openness of a media culture, in that some, or many, of its cultural patterns are shared with other cultures.

This seems to stand in contradiction to some of the foregoing, where patterns of communicative action have formed the central point of the argument. Not only in the general definition of communication, but also in considering the role of communication networks of the communicative articulation of communitizations, it has always been a matter of processes of action, or practices. The contradiction is resolved by reference to the framing *perspective of media and communication studies*: if one treats the discipline of media and communication studies as defined by the way it approaches socio-cultural phenomena in terms of mediation by communication media, then it is the practice of mediation itself that moves into the centre of empirical study. It is also thereby an analysis of people's communicative action which forms the core of the study of media and communications.

Here we need to link the definition of patterns to the categories of communication networks, or of communicative figurations. Methodologically, it is possible to treat both as concepts which deal with the patterned structure of communicative action: if we describe communicative networks, then ultimately we reconstruct structures of communicative connectivity that are more or less permanently generated by communicative action. The patterning of communicative action is described in terms of its communicative relationships. What pattern of communicative relation characterizes the life of a person from the standpoint of that person? How can we grasp the communicative relationships of a particular group of people? Questions such as these form the *point of departure* in the study of media cultures. Likewise this focus upon the patterns in communicative networks must always be placed in the context in which such communicative networking occurs. In this way one is confronted with substantive questions of communication (what is the pattern of discourse?) as well as questions of human perception and reality construction (what patterns of thought can be identified?). On this basis it becomes possible to understand patterns as communicative figurations.

Transcultural Comparisons

Following on from these points, we finally need to consider how the comparative study of media cultures should be conducted.

Many elements that we intuit to be specific to a media culture can only be made more precise through comparison with other media cultures. It should be evident from the arguments advanced in this book that a rather more complex analytical framework is required than that typical of much of the comparative media research so far done. Many such investigations display a kind of 'territorial essentialism', even when a definite effort is made to develop a systematic international framework (Curran and Park 2000; Thussu 2010). In these studies the state or national culture forms the prime point of reference, and we can generally refer to them as the international or intercultural approach to comparative media studies (Hepp and Couldry 2010).

What is problematic in such studies is not that particular aspects of media communication are linked to the state and so confined to a territorial framework. The state does remain an important focus for work dealing with political communication, where the focus falls naturally upon a national and therefore territorial decision-making process. Nonetheless, in the comparative study of media there remains a tendency to 'essentialize' this relationship between the state, (political) media systems, the media market and media culture in a binary comparative model. Then the comparative approach to media cultures becomes *essentially* the comparative definition of the nature of 'German', 'French' or 'English' media culture, for example.

A 'territorial essentialism' is problematic from the viewpoint presented in this book since, as we have argued, media cultures do not present themselves neatly divided among national 'boxes'. If we are studying cultures of mediatization in general, then we are confronted with much more complex entities. Certainly media cultures do have something to do with territorialization, understood as a particular process in the articulation or construction of meaning. But they also involve deterritorialization, since contemporary cultural forms are no longer constitutively related to any one particular territory. Thinking 'in containers' here becomes problematic.

Where then should one begin with a comparative analysis? The answer is to employ a new comparative semantics, what we can call a 'transcultural perspective'. This should not be taken as suggesting that we direct ourselves *exclusively* to cultural forms that exist 'beyond' or 'across' cultures. Wolfgang Welsch (1999) has used the term 'transcultural' to identify the way in which important present-day cultural phenomena cannot be broken down to questions of traditional culture localized in particular countries. Instead, many contemporary cultural forms are characterized by the way that they are articulated across various territories, and exist *alongside* territorialized cultural forms. One could call to mind here certain management cultures, as well as popular cultures or the other forms of deterritorial cultural thickenings discussed above.

Given the question 'how should one compare?', a transcultural approach breaks down the binary choice between international and intercultural, without excluding state and nation as possible points of comparative reference. A transcultural approach does not suppose media cultures to be necessarily and exclusively tied to territorial states. Instead, it focuses attention upon cultures of mediatization as specific thickenings in increasingly global connectivities. A comparative semantics of this kind seeks to highlight the specific nature of these thickenings, as well as the relationships existing among them.

It is therefore a question of how comparisons are made in the context of any particular study. Transcultural comparison does not begin with the binarism of a national comparison, in which each cultural pattern is understood to be an expression of a national media culture, but rather opens up a diverse process of comparison. As Glaser and Strauss (1967) explained, the elaboration of a 'substantive' theory is generally comparative: different 'cases' – interviews, media products, diaries, observational notes, and so forth – are all compared with each other. The aim is to develop the principal categories of a new theory in an ongoing process via the examination of various cases.

This is exactly the same process realized in transcultural comparative research. Without the data first being aggregated on a national-territorial basis, the cases from various cultural contexts are compared the one with the other. In this way one can obtain a system of categories that describes not simply national differences, but more general common factors and differences in cultural patterns. This approach makes greater complexity of analysis possible, and opens the way to the identification of media-cultural thickenings that can assume very different forms.

In practice, such comparisons can be realized as follows:

- Data must first be organized into cases formed around social entities: for example, by person (combining various data sources relating to one person, such as interviews, media diaries), by organization (combining various organizational data sources such as interviews with various persons, transcripts of group discussions, observational notes) or by similar units.

- Secondly, the process of transcultural comparison of these cases begins with a categorization of different cultural patterns. The main point here is to retain openness in mapping different cultural forms. Associated with this, care must be taken in determining whether a particular cultural pattern is specific to one nation, is transcultural but stable, or whether it is characteristic of a deterritorialized communitization, such as a diaspora, a political movement or a religious movement.

- Thirdly, the results of such comparison are structured according to the choice of diverse cultural thickenings of interest within the research framework, according to a territorial (region or nation) or a deterritorialized level (different kinds of deterritorialized translocal communitizations); or whether they exist at a level that persists beyond these levels.

This kind of comparative approach makes it possible to study different kinds of cultural thickenings beyond an essentialized national framework. In this kind of comparison media culture becomes accessible as an articulation of diverse patterns.

7

———

Prospect

As has been emphasized many times in the foregoing, this book cannot provide any definitive answer to the question: what is the nature of today's media cultures? Perhaps no such book will be written in the near future with the kind of full response to this question that might be hoped for. The contemporary mediatization of popular culture, of political culture, of religious culture, of national culture, of the culture of diaspora, and so forth, is too varied to be brought together in a unitary manner. The aim of this book is much more modest. It seeks to formulate some ideas in terms of which theoretical and empirical research of media culture can be approached. The concept of media cultures as cultures of mediatization does *not* therefore aim to be a *finished theory*, but is rather a call to develop an empirically founded theorization of the manner *in which our cultures are changing with the advance of mediatization.*

The set of concepts that I have elaborated is certainly comparatively simple if one considers the structures that, for example, systems theory has developed. But I hope that this will serve to promote practical analysis, in turn leading to a more complex, empirically founded theorization.

I have been concerned here to show that the mediatization of culture does *not* mean that today's media cultures function according to a unitary media logic. Of course, media as institutions and reifications alter our communicative action, and with that our articulation of reality. This is, however, made manifest in different contexts in different ways. And so it seems to make more sense to talk of the moulding forces of individual media, which come together with others and can then only be contextually investigated. There are several conceptual points of departure for such an investigation: the concept of the mediatized world as an everyday manifestation of mediatization; the concept of communicative networking to describe structures of communication in these mediatized worlds; and the concept of communicative figuration to provide an overarching framework for media communication. It has also been argued – in relation to the subjective level of media culture – that we need to keep in view questions of translocal communitization in both their territorial and deterritorialized variants.

I would like to come back here to a point raised at the very beginning. This concerns the *critical stance* taken with respect to the contemporary change of media cultures. This is of course central to the theory of the culture industry developed by Adorno and Horkheimer. Is it enough to simply describe particular circumstances, or should we adopt a critical stance? The question is easily posed, but not so easily answered. How is it possible to adopt a critical stance in the empirical study of media cultures without simply imposing our own normative framework, our own cultural pattern? There is likewise no context-free answer to this question. Nonetheless, in closing there are three basic principles that can be outlined which might enable us to develop a multiperspectival critique of today's cultures of mediatization.

The first principle is the necessity of *focusing upon the constructive process of cultural articulation*. As emphasized before, in cultures of mediatization 'the media' are themselves constructed through particular cultural patterns as 'central'. Alongside that are other patterns of 'centralization' within media cultures: for example, that of 'national territories' in national media cultures, of 'deterritorialized religious entities' in transnational religious movements, of the 'globally popular' among popular-cultural communitizations. The non-essentialist approach to the analysis of media cultures outlined in this book permits such implicit processes of 'centralization' to be brought into focus, in that major variables are not initially posited.

The second principle can be seen as a *focus upon the relation of cultural patterns to questions of power*. I have repeatedly talked of the power of communication. Emphasis upon the 'centralizing' aspects of the construction processes of cultural articulation raises questions of power, since the creation of a 'cultural centre' implies cultural power. But even beyond these 'centralizing features' there are patterns in cultures of mediatization that relate to power: particular cultural patterns open up possibilities of hegemony and domination; others do not. Besides that, the institutionalization and reification of communicative action in media technologies raise the question of the extent to which particular elements of communicative power can be rendered permanent. Correspondingly, this second principle impels us to think about the degree to which the cultural patterns so described are linked to power relationships within media cultures, and for whom these are of use. Also important is the question of the extent to which this pattern opens up particular spaces of everyday action, or closes them off.

The third principle can be called the integration of all these findings in a *multiperspectival critique*. A comparative approach yields different perspectives upon cultures of mediatization, and upon their processes of cultural articulation and power relationships. But the aim of this analysis cannot be the reduction of this complexity to any one particular meaning. Instead, an analytic description should render diverse media cultures accessible in their power-related inconsistencies. And this should be especially true of transcultural comparative research.

As Douglas Kellner has noted (1995b: 3), a general approach to media cultures is risky, given its complexity. It would therefore be wrong to read the arguments advanced here as though they were the only ones possible in this field. Other approaches place emphasis on other important aspects. Nonetheless, I would like to argue that the perspective upon media cultures developed here – as cultures of mediatization – is a highly productive point of departure for understanding the relationship between media-communicative and socio-cultural change. My hope is that this book stimulates the development of research as well as a critical public discourse in a like direction.

References

Adorno, Theodor W. (1975) 'Culture Industry Reconsidered'. *New German Critique*, 6, pp. 12–19.

Aksoy, Asu and Robins, Kevin (2000) 'Thinking across Spaces: Transnational Television from Turkey'. *European Journal of Cultural Studies*, 3 (3), pp. 343–65.

Altheide, David L. (2004) 'Media Logic and Political Communication'. *Political Communication*, 21 (3), pp. 293–6.

Altheide, David L. and Snow, Robert P. (1979) *Media Logic*. Beverly Hills, CA: Sage.

Altheide, David L. and Snow, Robert P. (1988) 'Toward a Theory of Mediation'. In James A. Anderson (eds) *Communication Yearbook 11*. Newbury Park, CA: Sage, pp. 194–223.

Altheide, David L. and Snow, Robert P. (1991) *Media Worlds in the Postjournalism Era*. New York: Aldine.

Anderson, Benedict (1983) *Imagined Communities: Reflections on the Origins and Spread of Nationalism*. New York: Verso.

Ang, Ien (1996) *Living Room Wars: Rethinking Media Audiences for a Postmodern World*. London and New York: Routledge.

Asp, Kent (1990) 'Medialization, Media Logic and Mediarchy'. *Nordicom Review*, 11 (2), pp. 47–50.

Atton, Chris (2002) *Alternative Media*. London, Thousand Oaks, CA and New Delhi: Sage.

Atton, Chris (2004) *An Alternative Internet: Radical Media, Politics and Creativity*. Edinburgh: Edinburgh University Press.

Averbeck-Lietz, Stefanie (2011) 'Mediatization and Communication History: Looking Backwards to First Modernity with Classical Readings: Max Weber, Ferdinand Tönnies and Ernest Manheim'. Paper presented at the conference Mediatized Worlds: Culture and Society in a Media Age, 14–15 April 2011, University of Bremen, Haus der Wissenschaft, Bremen, Germany.

References

Baacke, Dieter, Sander, Uwe and Vollbrecht, Ralf (1991) *Medienwelten Jugendlicher*. Opladen: Leske + Budrich.

Bailey, Olga G., Georgiou, Myria and Harindranth, Ramaswami (eds.) (2007) *Transnational Lives and the Media: Re-imagining Diasporas*. New York: Palgrave Macmillan.

Bailey, Olga G., Cammaerts, Bart and Carpentier, Nico (2008) *Understanding Alternative Media*. Maidenhead, Berks: Open University Press.

Barker, Chris (2002) *Making Sense of Cultural Studies: Central Problems and Cirtical Debates*. London, Thousand Oaks, CA and New Delhi: Sage.

Bauman, Zygmunt (2001) *Community*. Cambridge: Polity.

Bauman, Zygmunt (2007) *Consuming Life*. Cambridge: Polity.

Baym, Nancy K. (2000) *Tune In, Log On: Soaps, Fandom, and On-Line Community*. London, Thousand Oaks, CA and New Delhi: Sage.

Beck, Klaus (2006) *Computervermittelte Kommunikation im Internet*. Munich: Oldenbourg.

Beck, Ulrich (1987) 'Beyond Status and Class: Will There Be an Individualized Class Society?' In Volker Meja, Dieter Misgeld and Nico Stehr (eds.) *Modern German Sociology*. New York: Columbia University Press, pp. 340–55.

Beck, Ulrich (1996) *The Reinvention of Politics: Rethinking Modernity in the Global Social Order*. Cambridge: Polity.

Beck, Ulrich and Beck-Gernsheim, Elisabeth (2001) *Individualization: Institutionalized Individualism and Its Social and Political Consequences*. London and New Delhi: Sage.

Bemerburg, Ivonne and Niederbacher, Arne (eds.) (2007) *Die Globalisierung und ihre Kritik(er): Zum Stand der aktuellen Globalisierungsdebatte*. Wiesbaden: VS.

Beniger, James R. (1986) *The Control Revolution: Technological and Economic Origins of the Information Society*. Cambridge, MA and London: Harvard University Press.

Berg, Matthias (2010) 'Communicative Mobility and Mobile Work: The Management of Everyday Life and Communication Networks in a Mediatized World'. In Joachim R. Höflich, Georg F. Kircher, Christine Linke and Isabel Schlote (eds.) *Mobile Media and the Change of Everyday Life*. Berlin: Peter Lang, pp. 193–212.

Berger, Peter L. and Luckmann, Thomas (1967) *The Social Construction of Reality: A Treatise in the Sociology of Knowledge*. London: Penguin.

Berger, Peter L. and Pullberg, Stanley (1965) 'Reification and the Sociological Critique of Consciousness'. *History and Theory*, 4 (2), pp. 196–211.

Berker, Thomas, Hartmann, Maren, Punie, Yves and Ward, Katie (eds.) (2006) *Domestication of Media and Technology*. London: Open University Press.

Beth, Hanno and Pross, Harry (1976) *Einführung in die Kommunikationswissenschaft*. Stuttgart: Kohlhammer.

References

Bird, Elizabeth (2003) *The Audience in Everyday Life: Living in a Media World.* New York and London: Routledge.

Bösch, Frank (2011) *Mediengeschichte. Vom asiatischen Buchdruck zum Fernsehen.* Frankfurt: Campus.

Brecht, Bertolt (1979) 'Radio as a Means of Communication: A Talk on the Function of Radio'. *Screen*, 20 (31–4), pp. 24–8.

Bromley, Roger (2000) *Narratives for a New Belonging: Diasporic Cultural Fictions.* Edinburgh: Edinburgh University Press.

Bühl, Walter L. (1986) 'Kultur als System'. In Friedhelm Neidhart, Rainer M. Lepsius, M. Rainer and Johannes Weiß (eds.) *Kultur und Gesellschaft: Kölner Zeitschrift für Soziologie und Sozialpsychologie*, Sonderheft 27. Opladen: Westdeutscher, pp. 118–44.

Castells, Manuel (1997) *The Power of Identity. The Information Age: Economy, Society and Culture, Vol. 2.* Oxford: Blackwell.

Castells, Manuel (2000) *The Rise of the Network Society. The Information Age: Economy, Society and Culture, Vol. 1.* Second edition. Oxford: Blackwell.

Castells, Manuel (2001) *The Internet Galaxy: Reflections on the Internet, Business, and Society.* Oxford: Oxford University Press.

Clifford, James (1994) 'Diaspora'. *Cultural Anthropology*, 9 (3), pp. 302–38.

Cohen, Robin (2008) *Global Diasporas: An Introduction.* Second edition. London: Routledge.

Couldry, Nick (2006) 'Transvaluing Media Studies: Or, Beyond the Myth of the Mediated Centre'. In James Curran and David Morley (eds.) *Media and Cultural Theory.* London: Routledge, pp. 177–94.

Couldry, Nick (2008) 'Mediatization or Mediation? Alternative Understandings of the Emergent Space of Digital Storytelling'. *New Media & Society*, 10 (3), pp. 373–91.

Couldry, Nick (2009) 'Does "the Media" Have a Future?' *European Journal of Communication*, 24 (4), pp. 437–50.

Couldry, Nick (2012) *Media, Society, World: Social Theory and Digital Media Practice.* Cambridge: Polity.

Couldry, Nick and Curran, James (eds.) (2003) *Contesting Media Power: Alternative Media in a Networked World.* London: Rowman & Littlefield.

Curran, James and Park, Myung-Jin (eds.) (2000) *De-Westernizing Media Studies.* London and New York: Routledge.

Dayan, Daniel (1999) 'Media and Diasporas'. In Jostein Gripsrud (eds) *Television and Common Knowledge.* London and New York: Routledge, pp. 18–33.

Deterding, Sebastian (2008) 'Virtual Communities'. In Ronald Hitzler, Anne Honer and Michaela Pfadenhauer (eds.) *Posttraditionale Gemeinschaften: Theoretische und ethnografische Erkundungen.* Wiesbaden: VS, pp. 115–31.

Dörner, Andreas (2006) 'Political Culture and Media Culture: Constructing Political Identities in the US and Germany'. In William Uricchio and Susanne Kinnebrock (eds.) *Media Cultures.* Heidelberg: Winter, pp. 41–8.

References

du Gay, Paul, Hall, Stuart, Janes, Linda, Mackay, Hugh and Negus, Keith (1997) *Doing Cultural Studies: The Story of the Sony Walkman*. London: Sage.

Elias, Norbert (1978) *What is Sociology?* London: Hutchinson.

Elias, Norbert (1991) *The Symbol Theory*. London: Sage.

Elias, Norbert (2000) *The Civilizing Process*. Oxford and Malden, MA: Wiley-Blackwell.

Everitt, Dave and Mills, Simon (2009) 'Cultural Anxiety 2.0'. *Media, Culture & Society*, 31 (5), pp. 749–68.

Faulstich, Werner (1998) 'Medienkultur'. In Werner Faulstich (ed.) *Grundwissen Medien*. Third edition. Munich: Wilhelm Fink (UTB), pp. 99–105.

Favell, Adrian (2008) *Eurostars and Eurocities: Free Movement and Mobility in an Integrating Europe*. Malden, MA: Blackwell.

Featherstone, Mike (1991) *Consumer Culture and Postmodernism*. London: Sage.

Fiske, John (1987) *Television Culture*. London and New York: Routledge.

Fornäs, Johan (2000) 'The Crucial In Between: The Centrality of Mediation in Cultural Studies'. *European Journal of Cultural Studies*, 3 (1), pp. 45–65.

Foucault, Michel (1991) *Discipline and Punish: The Birth of the Prison*. London: Penguin.

Foucault, Michel (1994) *The Order of Things*. New York: Random House.

García Canclini, Néstor (1995) *Hybrid Cultures: Strategies for Entering and Leaving Modernity*. Minneapolis: University of Minnesota Press.

Gauntlett, David (2007) 'Media Studies 2.0'. *Theory.org.uk, http://www.theory.org.uk/mediastudies2.htm* (last accessed 15 March 2011).

Gauntlett, David (2011) *Making is Connecting: The Social Meaning of Creativity, from DIY and Knitting to YouTube and Web 2.0*. Cambridge: Polity.

Georgiou, Myria (2006) *Diaspora, Identity and the Media: Diasporic Transnationalism and Mediated Spatialities*. Cresskill, NJ: Hampton Press.

Giddens, Anthony (1984) *The Constitution of Society*. Cambridge: Polity.

Giddens, Anthony (1990) *The Consequences of Modernity*. Cambridge: Polity.

Gillespie, Marie (1995) *Television, Ethnicity and Cultural Change*. London and New York: Routledge.

Gillespie, Marie (2000) 'Transnational Communications and Diaspora Communities'. In Simon Cottle (ed.) *Ethnic Minorities and the Media*. Buckingham: Open University Press, pp. 164–78.

Ginsburg, Faye D., Abu-Lughod, Lila and Larkin, Brian (eds.) (2002) *Media Worlds: Anthropology on New Terrain*. Berkeley: California University Press.

Glaser, Barney G. (2007) 'Doing Formal Theory'. In Antony Bryant and Kathy Charmaz (eds.) *Grounded Theory*. Los Angeles: Sage, pp. 97–113.

Glaser, Barney G. and Strauss, Anselm L. (1967) *Discovery of Grounded Theory: Strategies for Qualitative Research*. New Brunswick, NJ: AldineTransaction.

Grossberg, Lawrence, Wartella, Ellen and Withney, D. Charles (1998) *MediaMaking: Mass Media in a Popular Culture*. London: Sage.

References

Groth, Otto (1948) *Die Geschichte der deutschen Zeitungswissenschaft: Probleme und Methoden*. Munich: Weinmayer.

Groth, Otto (1960) *Die unerkannte Kulturmacht: Grundlegung der Zeitungswissenschaft (Periodik). Band 1: Das Wesen des Werkes*. Berlin: de Gruyter.

Gurak, Laura J. (2004) 'Internet Studies in the 21st Century'. In David Gauntlett and Ross Horsley (eds.) *Web.Studies*. Second edition. London: Arnold, pp. 24–33.

Hall, Stuart (1980) 'Encoding/Decoding'. In Stuart Hall, Dorothy Hobson, Andrew Lowe, Andrew and Paul Willis (eds.) *Culture, Media, Language: Working Papers in Cultural Studies 1972–79*. London and New York: Routledge, pp. 128–38.

Hall, Stuart (1992) 'The Question of Cultural Identity'. In Stuart Hall, David Held and Tony McGrew (eds.) *Modernity and Its Futures*. Cambridge: Polity, pp. 273–6.

Hall, Stuart (1997) 'The Centrality of Culture: Notes on the Cultural Revolutions of Our Time'. In Kenneth Thompson (ed.) *Media and Cultural Regulation*. London: Sage, pp. 207–38.

Hannerz, Ulf (1992) *Cultural Complexity: Studies on the Social Organization of Meaning*. New York: Columbia University Press.

Harbord, Janet (2002) *Film Cultures*. London: Sage.

Hartmann, Maren (2006) 'The Triple Articulation of ICTs: Media as Technological Objects, Symbolic Environments and Individual Texts'. In Thomas Berker, Maren Hartmann, Yves Punie and Katie Ward (eds.) *Domestication of Media and Technology*. London: Open University Press, pp. 80–102.

Hartmann, Maren (2009) 'The Changing Urban Landscapes of Media Consumption and Production'. *European Journal of Communication*, 24 (4), pp. 421–36.

Hasebrink, Uwe (2003) 'Nutzungsforschung'. In Günter Bentele, Hans-Bernd Brosius and Otfried Jarren (eds) *Öffentliche Kommunikation: Handbuch Kommunikations- und Medienwissenschaft*. Wiesbaden: Westdeutscher Verlag, pp. 101–27.

Hasebrink, Uwe and Hanna Domeyer (2010) 'Zum Wandel von Informationsrepertoires in konvergierenden Medienumgebungen'. In Maren Hartmann and Andreas Hepp (eds.) *Die Mediatisierung der Alltagswelt*. Wiesbaden: VS, pp. 49–64.

Hasebrink, Uwe and Jutta Popp (2006) 'Media Repertoires as a Result of Selective Media Use: A Conceptual Approach to the Analysis of Patterns of Exposure'. *Communications*, 31 (2), pp. 369–87.

Henscheid, Eckhard (2001) *Alle 756 Kulturen: Eine Bilanz*. Frankfurt: Zweitausendeins.

Hepp, Andreas (1998) *Fernsehaneignung und Alltagsgespräche: Fernsehnutzung aus der Perspektive der Cultural Studies*. Opladen: Westdeutscher.

References

Hepp, Andreas (2004) *Netzwerke der Medien: Medienkulturen und Globalisierung*. Wiesbaden: VS.

Hepp, Andreas (2006) *Transkulturelle Kommunikation*. Konstanz: UVK (UTB).

Hepp, Andreas (2008) 'Translocal Media Cultures: Networks of the Media and Globalization'. In Andreas Hepp, Friedrich Krotz, Shaun Moores and Carsten Winter (eds.) *Connectivity, Networks and Flows: Conceptualizing Contemporary Communications*. Cresskill, NJ: Hampton Press, pp. 33–58.

Hepp, Andreas (2009) 'Differentiation: Mediatization and Cultural Change'. In Knut Lundby (ed.) *Mediatization: Concept, Changes, Consequences*. New York: Peter Lang, pp. 135–54.

Hepp, Andreas and Couldry, Nick (2010) 'What Should Comparative Media Research be Comparing? Towards a Transcultural Approach to "Media Cultures"'. In Daya Kishan Thussu (ed.) *Internationalizing Media Studies: Impediments and Imperatives*. London: Routledge, pp. 32–47.

Hepp, Andreas and Couldry, Nick (2010) 'Media Events in Globalized Media Cultures'. In Nick Couldry, Andreas Hepp and Friedrich Krotz (eds.) *Media Events in a Global Age*. London: Routledge, pp. 1–20.

Hepp, Andreas and Krönert, Veronika (2010) 'Religious Media Events: The Catholic "World Youth Day" as an Example for the Mediatization and Individualization of Religion'. In Nick Couldry, Andreas Hepp and Friedrich Krotz (eds.) *Media Events in a Global Age*. London: Routledge, pp. 265–82.

Hepp, Andreas and Vogelgesang, Waldemar (2005) 'Medienkritik der Globalisierung: Die kommunikative Vernetzung der globalisierungskritischen Bewegung'. In Andreas Hepp, Friedrich Krotz and Carsten Winter (eds.) *Globalisierung der Medien*. Wiesbaden: VS, pp. 229–60.

Hepp, Andreas, Bozdag, Cigdem and Suna, Laura (2012) 'Mediatized Migrants: Media Cultures and Communicative Networking in the Diaspora'. In Leopoldina Fortunati, Raul Pertierra and Jane Vincent (eds.) *Migrations, Diaspora, and Information Technology in Global Societies*. London: Routledge, pp. 172–88.

Hickethier, Knut (2003) 'Medienkultur'. In Günter Bentele, Hans-Bernd Brosius and Otfried Jarren (eds.) *Öffentliche Kommunikation: Handbuch Kommunikations- und Medienwissenschaft*. Wiesbaden: Westdeutscher, pp. 435–57.

Hitzler, Ronald (1998) 'Posttraditionale Vergemeinschaftung. Über neue Formen der Sozialbindung'. *Berliner Debatte INITIAL*, 9 (1), pp. 81–89.

Hitzler, Ronald (2000) '"Ein bisschen Spaß muss sein!": Zur Konstruktion kultureller Erlebniswelten'. In Winfried Gebhardt, Ronald Hitzler and Michaela Pfadenhauer (eds.) *Events: Soziologie des Außergewöhnlichen*. Opladen: Leske + Budrich, pp. 401–12.

Hitzler, Ronald (2002), *'Globalisierungsgegner': Eine 'bewegte Szene'?* Dortmund: Unveröffentlichtes Manuskript.

Hitzler, Ronald (2007) 'Phänomenologie'. In Renate Buber and Hartmut H.

References

Holzmüller (eds.) *Qualitative Marktforschung: Konzepte – Methoden – Analysen*. Wiesbaden: Gabler, pp. 81–92.

Hitzler, Ronald (2008a) 'Brutstätten posttraditionaler Vergemeinschaftung'. In Ronald Hitzler, Anne Honer and Michaela Pfadenhauer (eds.) *Posttraditionale Gemeinschaften: Theoretische und ethnographische Erkundungen*. Wiesbaden: VS, pp. 55–72.

Hitzler, Ronald (2008b) 'Von der Lebenswelt zu den Erlebniswelten: Ein phänomenologischer Weg in soziologische Gegenwartsfragen'. In Jürgen Raab, Michaela Pfadenhauer, Peter Stegmaier, Jochen Dreher and Bernt Schnettler (eds.) *Phänomenologie und Soziologie: Theoretische Positionen, aktuelle Problemfelder und empirische Umsetzungen*. Wiesbaden: VS, pp. 131–40.

Hitzler, Ronald (2010) *Eventisierung*. Wiesbaden: VS.

Hitzler, Ronald and Eberle, Thomas (2003) 'Phänomenologische Lebensweltanalyse'. In Uwe Flick, Ernst von Kardorff and Ines Steinke (eds.) *Qualitative Forschung: Ein Handbuch*. Second edition. Hamburg: Rowohlt, pp. 109–18.

Hitzler, Ronald and Honer, Anne (1984) 'Lebenswelt – Milieu – Situation: Terminologische Vorschläge zur theoretischen Verständigung'. *Kölner Zeitschrift für Soziologie und Sozialpsychologie*, 36 (1), pp. 56–74.

Hitzler, Ronald and Honer, Anne (1994) 'Bastelexistenz: Über subjektive Konsequenzen der Individualisierung'. In Ulrich Beck and Elisabeth Beck-Gernsheim (eds.) *Riskante Freiheiten*. Frankfurt: Suhrkamp, pp. 307–15.

Hitzler, Ronald and Möll, Gerd (2012) 'Eingespielte Transzendenzen: Zur Mediatisierung des Welterlebens am Beispiel des Pokerns'. In Friedrich Krotz and Andreas Hepp (eds) *Mediatisierte Welten: Forschungsfelder und Beschreibungsansätze*. Wiesbaden: VS, pp. 257–80.

Hitzler, Ronald and Niederbacher, Arne (2010) *Leben in Szenen: Formen juveniler Vergemeinschaftung heute*. Third fully revised edition. Wiesbaden: VS.

Hjarvard, Stig (2004) 'From Bricks to Bytes: The Mediatization of a Global Toy Industry'. In Ib Bondebjerg and Peter Golding (eds.) *European Culture and the Media*. Bristol: Intellect, pp. 43–63.

Hjarvard, Stig (2008) 'The Mediatization of Society: A Theory of the Media as Agents of Social and Cultural Change'. *Nordicom Review*, 29 (2), pp. 105–34.

Hjarvard, Stig (2009) 'Soft Individualism: Media and the Changing Social Character'. In Knut Lundby (ed.) *Mediatization: Concept, Changes, Consequences*. New York: Peter Lang, pp. 159–77.

Höflich, Joachim R. (2005) 'A Certain Sense of Place: Mobile Communication and Local Orientation'. In Kristóf Nyíri (ed.) *A Sense of Place: The Global and the Local in Mobile Communication*. Vienna: Passagen, pp. 159–68.

Holly, Werner, Kühn, Peter and Püschel, Ulrich (1984) 'Für einen "sinnvollen" Handlungsbegriff in der linguistischen Pragmatik'. *Zeitschrift für Germanistische Linguistik*, 12, pp. 275–312.

Holzer, Boris (2006) *Netzwerke*. Münster: Transcript.

References

Hoover, Stewart (2006) *Religion in the Media Age*. London and New York: Routledge.

Horkheimer, Max and Adorno, Theodor W. (1986) *Dialectic of Enlightenment*. London: Verso.

Hug, Theo and Friesen, Norm (2009) 'The Mediatic Turn: Exploring Concepts for Media Pedagogy'. In Knut Lundby (ed.) *Mediatization: Concept, Changes, Consequences*. New York: Peter Lang, pp. 63–83.

Illich, Ivan (1973) *Tools for Conviviality*. New York: Harper and Row.

Illich, Ivan (1993) *In the Vineyard of the Text: Commentary to Hugh's 'Didascalicon'*. Chicago and London: University of Chicago Press.

Innis, Harold A. (1950) *Empire and Communications*. Oxford: Clarendon.

Innis, Harold A. (1951) *The Bias of Communication*. Toronto: University of Toronto Press.

Jenkins, Henry (2006a) *Convergence Culture: Where Old and New Media Collide*. New York: New York University Press.

Jenkins, Henry (2006b) *Fans, Bloggers and Gamers: Essays on Participatory Culture*. New York: New York University Press.

Johnson, Richard (1986) 'What is Cultural Studies Anyway?' *Social Text*, 16, pp. 38–80.

Jones, Steven G. (1997) 'Introduction'. In Steven G. Jones (ed.) *Virtual Culture: Identity and Communication in Cybersociety*. London: Sage, pp. 1–6.

Jong, Wilma de, Shaw, Martin and Stammers, Neil (2005) 'Introduction'. In Wilma Jong, Martin Shaw and Neil Stammers (eds.) *Global Activism, Global Media*. London: Pluto Press, pp. 1–14.

Katz, Elihu and Lazarsfeld, Paul F. (1955) *Personal Influence: The Part Played by People in Mass Communication*. New York: Free Press.

Keller, Reiner (2008) 'Welcome to the Pleasuredome? Konstanzen und Flüchtigkeiten der gefühlten Vergemeinschaftung'. In Ronald Hitzler, Anne Honer and Michaela Pfadenhauer (eds.) *Posttraditionale Gemeinschaften: Theoretische und ethnographische Erkundungen*. Wiesbaden: VS, pp. 89–111.

Kellner, Douglas (1995a) 'Media Communications vs Cultural Studies: Overcoming the Divide'. *Communication Theory*, 5 (1), pp. 162–77.

Kellner, Douglas (1995b) *Media Culture: Cultural Studies, Identity and Politics between the Modern and the Postmodern*. London and New York: Routledge.

Keppler, Angela (1994) *Tischgespräche: Über Formen kommunikativer Vergemeinschaftung am Beispiel der Konversation in Familien*. Frankfurt: Suhrkamp.

Kepplinger, Hans Matthias (2002) 'Mediatization of Politics: Theory and Data'. *Journal of Communication*, 52, pp. 972–86.

Klein, Naomi (2000) *No Logo®: Taking Aim at the Brand Bullies*. London: Flamingo.

Knoblauch, Hubert (1989) 'Das unsichtbare neue Zeitalter: "New Age",

References

privatisierte Religion und kultische Milieus'. *Kölner Zeitschrift für Soziologie und Sozialpsychologie*, 41 (3), pp. 504–25.

Knoblauch, Hubert (2008) 'Kommunikationsgemeinschaften: Überlegungen zur kommunikativen Konstruktion einer Sozialform'. In Ronald Hitzler, Anne Honer, Anne and Michaela Pfadenhauer (eds.) *Posttraditionale Gemeinschaften: Theoretische und ethnographische Erkundungen*. Wiesbaden: VS, pp. 73–88.

Knoblauch, Hubert (2009) *Populäre Religion: Auf dem Weg in eine spirituelle Gesellschaft*. Frankfurt: Campus Wissenschaft.

Knoblauch, Hubert (2011) 'Communication Culture, Communicative Action and Mediatization'. Paper presented at the conference Mediatized Worlds: Culture and Society in a Media Age, 14–15 April 2011, University of Bremen, Haus der Wissenschaft, Bremen, Germany.

Krotz, F. (2001) *Die Mediatisierung kommunikativen Handelns: Der Wandel von Alltag und sozialen Beziehungen, Kultur und Gesellschaft durch die Medien*. Opladen: Westdeutscher Verlag.

Krotz, Friedrich (2005) *Neue Theorien entwickeln: Eine Einführung in die Grounded Theory, die Heuristische Sozialforschung und die Ethnographie anhand von Beispielen aus der Kommunikationsforschung*. Cologne: Halem.

Krotz, Friedrich (2007) *Mediatisierung: Fallstudien zum Wandel von Kommunikation*. Wiesbaden: VS.

Krotz, Friedrich (2008a) 'Handlungstheorien und Symbolischer Interaktionismus als Grundlage kommunikationswissenschaftlicher Forschung'. In Carsten Winter, Andreas Hepp and Friedrich Krotz (eds.) *Theorien der Kommunikations- und Medienwissenschaft: Grundlegende Diskussionen, Forschungsfelder und Theorieentwicklungen*. Wiesbaden: VS, pp. 29–47.

Krotz, Friedrich (2008b) 'Media Connectivity: Concepts, Conditions, and Consequences'. In Andreas Hepp, Friedrich Krotz, Shaun Moores and Carsten Winter (eds.) *Network, Connectivity and Flow: Conceptualizing Contemporary Communications*. Cresskill, NJ: Hampton Press, pp. 13–31.

Krotz, Friedrich (2009) 'Mediatization: A Concept With Which to Grasp Media and Societal Change'. In Knut Lundby (ed.) *Mediatization: Concept, Changes, Consequences*. New York: Peter Lang, pp. 19–38.

Krotz, Friedrich, Funken, Christiane, Hepp, Andreas and Jäckel, Michael (2008a) *Mediatisierte Welten: Kommunikation im medialen und gesellschaftlichen Wandel*. Application to the German Research Foundation for the establishment of a priority programme (*Schwerpunktprogramms*).

Krotz, Friedrich, Hepp, Andreas and Winter, Carsten (2008b) 'Einleitung: Theorien der Kommunikations- und Medienwissenschaft'. In Carsten Winter, Andreas Hepp and Friedrich Krotz (eds.) *Theorien der Kommunikations- und Medienwissenschaft: Grundlegende Diskussionen, Forschungsfelder und Theorieentwicklungen*. Wiesbaden: VS, pp. 9–27.

Kubicek, Herbert (1997) 'Das Internet auf dem Weg zum Massenmedium?

References

Ein Versuch, Lehren aus der Geschichte alter und neuer Medien zu ziehen'. In Raymund Werle and Christa Lang (eds.) *Modell Internet? Entwicklungsperspektiven neuer Kommunikationsnetze.* Frankfurt/New York: Campus, pp. 213–39.

Langenbucher, Wolfgang R. (1998) 'Einführung: Zu Person und Werk'. In Otto Groth (ed. Wolfgan R. Langenbucher) *Vermittelte Mitteilung: Ein journalistisches Modell der Massenkommunikation.* Munich: Fischer, pp. 151–86.

Lasswell, Harold D. (1961) 'The Structure and Function of Communication in Society'. In Wilbur Schramm (ed.) *Mass Communication.* Urbana, Chicago and London: Illinois University Press, pp. 117–30.

Latour, Bruno (1991) 'Technology is Society Made Durable'. In John Law (ed.) *A Sociology of Monsters: Essays on Power, Technology and Domination.* London: Routledge, pp. 103–31.

Latour, Bruno (1993) *We Have Never Been Modern.* Cambridge, MA: Harvard University Press.

Latour, Bruno (2007) *Reassembling the Social: An Introduction to Actor-Network-Theory.* Oxford: Oxford University Press.

Leavitt, Harold J. (1951) 'Some Effects of Certain Communication Patterns in Group Performance'. *Journal of Abnormal and Social Psychology,* 46 (1), pp. 38–50.

Lenk, Hans (1978) 'Handlung als Interpretationskonstrukt: Entwurf einer konstituenten- und beschreibungstheoretischen Handlungsphilosophie'. In Hans Lenk (ed.) *Handlungstheorien interdisziplinär II. Erster Halbband.* Munich: Fink, pp. 279–351.

Lerner, Daniel (1977) 'Towards a Communication Theory of Modernization: A Set of Considerations'. In Wilbur Schramm and Donald F. Roberts (eds.) *The Process and Effects of Mass Communication.* Fourth edition, fully revised. Urbana: University of Illinois Press, pp. 861–89.

Lievrouw, Leah A. (2001) 'New Media and the "Pluralization of Life-Worlds": A Role for Information in Social Differentiation'. *New Media & Society,* 3 (1), pp. 7–18.

Linke, Christine (2011) 'Being a Couple in a Media World: The Mediatization of Everyday Communication in Couple Relationships'. *Communications,* 36, pp. 91–111.

Lister, Martin, Kelly, Kieran, Dovey, Jon, Giddings, Seth and Grant, Iain (2009) *New Media: A Critical Introduction.* Second edition. London: Routledge.

Livingstone, Sonia M. (2009) 'On the Mediation of Everything'. *Journal of Communication,* 59 (1), pp. 1–18.

Löfgren, Orvar (2001) 'The Nation as Home or Motel? Metaphors of Media and Belonging'. *Sosiologisk Årbok,* 14 (1), pp. 1–34.

Loon, Joost van (2008) *Media Technology: Critical Perspectives.* Maidenhead: Open University Press.

References

Luckmann, Benita (1970) 'The Small Life-Worlds of Modern Man'. *Social Research*, 37 (4), pp. 580–96.

Luckmann, Thomas (1992) *Theorie des sozialen Handelns*. Berlin and New York: de Gruyter.

Luhmann, Niklas (1997) *Die Gesellschaft der Gesellschaft*. 2 vols. Frankfurt: Suhrkamp.

Luhmann, Niklas (2000) *The Reality of the Mass Media*. Cambridge: Polity.

Lull, James (1987) 'Audience Texts, and Contexts'. *Critical Studies in Mass Communication*, 4 (3), pp. 318–22.

Lundby, Knut (2006) 'Contested Communication: Mediating the Sacred'. In Johanna Sumiala-Seppänen, Knut Lundby and Raimo Salokangas (eds.) *Implications of the Sacred in (Post)Modern Media*. Gothenburg: Nordicom, pp. 43–62.

Lundby, Knut (2009) 'Media Logic: Looking for Social Interaction'. In Knut Lundby (ed.) *Mediatization: Concept, Changes, Consequences*. New York: Peter Lang, pp. 101–19.

McLuhan, Marshall (1962). *The Gutenberg Galaxy: The Making of Typographic Man*. Toronto: University of Toronto Press.

McLuhan, Marshall and Fiore, Quentin (1967) *The Medium is the Massage: An Inventory of Effects*. New York: Random House.

McLuhan, Marshall and Lapham, Lewis H. (1994) *Understanding Media: The Extensions of Man*. Cambridge, MA and London: MIT Press.

Maffesoli, Michel (1996) *The Time of the Tribes: The Decline of Individualism in Mass Society*. London, Thousand Oaks, CA and New Delhi: Sage.

Madianou, Mirca and Miller, Daniel (2011) *Migration and New Media: Transnational Families and Polymedia*. London: Routledge.

Manheim, Ernest (1933) *Die Träger der öffentlichen Meinung: Studien zur Soziologie der Öffentlichkeit*. Brünn: Rohrer.

Mann, Leon (1999) *Sozialpsychologie*. Weinheim: Beltz.

Martín-Barbero, Jesús (1993) *Communication, Culture, and Hegemony: From the Media to Mediations*. London, Thousand Oaks, CA and New Delhi: Sage.

Martín-Barbero, Jesús (2006) 'A Latin American Perspective on Communication/ Cultural Mediation'. *Global Media and Communication*, 2 (3), pp. 279–97.

Massey, Doreen (1994) *Space, Place and Gender*. Cambridge: Polity.

Mazzoleni, Gianpietro (2008a) 'Mediatization of Politics'. In Wolfgang Donsbach (ed.) *The International Encyclopedia of Communication, Vol. VII*. Oxford: Blackwell, pp. 3047–51.

Mazzoleni, Gianpietro (2008b) 'Mediatization of Society'. In Wolfgang Donsbach (ed.) *The International Encyclopedia of Communication, Vol VII*. Oxford: Blackwell, pp. 3052–5.

Mazzoleni, Gianpietro and Schulz, Winfried (1999) '"Mediatization" of Politics: A Challenge for Democracy?' *Political Communication*, 16, pp. 247–61.

References

Merten, Klaus (1994) 'Evolution der Kommunikation'. In Klaus Merten, Siegfried J. Schmidt and Siegfried Weischenberg (eds.) *Die Wirklichkeit der Medien: Eine Einführung in die Kommunikationswissenschaft.* Opladen: Westdeutscher, pp. 141–62.

Merten, Klaus, Schmidt, Siegfried J. and Weischenberg, Siegfried (eds.) (1994) *Die Wirklichkeit der Medien: Eine Einführung in die Kommunikationswissenschaft.* Opladen: Westdeutscher.

Meyen, Michael (2009) 'Medialisierung'. *Medien & Kommunikationswissenschaft,* 57 (1), pp. 23–38.

Meyrowitz, Joshua (1987) *No Sense of Place: Impact of Electronic Media on Social Behaviour.* Oxford: Oxford Unversity Press.

Meyrowitz, Joshua (1995) 'Medium Theory'. In David J. Crowley and David Mitchell (eds.) *Communication Theory Today.* Cambridge: Polity, pp. 50–77.

Meyrowitz, Joshua (2009) 'Medium Theory: An Alternative to the Dominant Paradigm of Media Effects'. In Robin L. Nabi and Mary Beth Oliver (eds.) *The Sage Handbook of Media Processes and Effects.* Thousand Oaks, CA: Sage, pp. 517–30.

Miller, Daniel and Slater, Don (2000) *The Internet: An Ethnographic Approach.* Oxford: Berg.

Monaco, James (1978) *Media Culture.* New York: Dell.

Moores, Shaun (2000) *Media and Everyday Life in Modern Society.* Edinburgh: Edinburgh University Press.

Moores, Shaun (2008) 'Conceptualizing Place in a World of Flows'. In Andreas Hepp, Friedrich Krotz, Shaun Moores and Carsten Winter (eds.) *Network, Connectivity and Flow: Conceptualizing Contemporary Communications.* Cresskill, NJ: Hampton Press, pp. 183–200.

Moran, Albert (2009) *TV Formats Worldwide: Localizing Global Programs.* Bristol: Intellect.

Morley, David (1998) 'So-Called Cultural Studies: Dead Ends and Reinvented Wheels'. *Cultural Studies,* 12, pp. 467–97.

Morley, David (2000) *Home Territories: Media, Mobility and Identity.* London and New York: Routledge.

Morley, David (2001) 'Belongings: Place, Space and Identity as Mediated World'. *European Journal of Cultural Studies,* 4 (4), pp. 425–48.

Morley, David (2007) *Media, Modernity and Technology: The Geography of the New.* London and New York: Routledge.

Morley, David (2009) 'For a Materialist, Non-Mediacentric Media Studies'. *Television & New Media,* 10 (1), pp. 114–16.

Morley, David and Silverstone, Roger (1991) 'Communication and Context: Ethnographic Perspectives on the Media Audience'. In Klaus Bruhn Jensen and Nicholas W. Jankowski (eds.) *Qualitative Methodologies for Mass Communication Research.* London and New York: Routledge, pp. 149–62.

References

Morris, Merrill and Ogan, Christine (1996) 'The Internet as Mass Medium'. *Journal of Communication*, 46 (1), pp. 39–50.

Müller-Doohm, Stefan (2008) 'Von der Kulturindustrieanalyse zur Idee partizipativer Öffentlichkeit: Reflexionsstufen kritischer Medientheorie'. In Carsten Winter, Andreas Hepp and Friedrich Krotz (eds.) *Theorien der Kommunikations- und Medienwissenschaft*. Wiesbaden: VS, pp. 49–63.

Naficy, Hamid (1993) *The Making of an Exile Culture*. London: University of Minnesota Press.

Nederveen Pieterse, Jan (1995) 'Globalization as Hybridization'. In Mike Featherstone, Scott Lash and Roland Robertson (eds.) *Global Modernities*. London: Sage, pp. 45–68.

Negus, Keith (1997) 'The Production of Culture'. In Paul du Gay (ed.) *Production of Culture/Cultures of Production*. London: Sage, pp. 67–104.

Negus, Keith (2006) 'Rethinking Creative Production Away from the Cultural Industries'. In James Curran and David Morley (eds.) *Media and Cultural Theory*. London and New York: Routledge, pp. 197–208.

Ong, Walter J. (2002) *Orality and Literacy*. London and New York: Routledge.

Pfadenhauer, Michaela (2008) 'Markengemeinschaften: Das Brand als "Totem" einer posttraditionalen Gemeinschaft'. In Ronald Hitzler, Anne Honer and Michaela Pfadenhauer (eds.) *Posttraditionale Gemeinschaften: Theoretische und ethnographische Erkundungen*. Wiesbaden: VS, pp. 214–27.

Pias, Claus (ed.) (1999) *Dreizehn Vorträge zur Medienkultur*. Weimar: Verlag und Datenbank für Geisteswissenschaften.

Pias, Claus, Vogl, Joseph, Engell, Lorenz, Fahle, Oliver and Neitzel, Britta (eds.) (1999) *Kursbuch Medienkultur: Die maßgeblichen Theorien von Brecht bis Baudrillard*. Stuttgart: Deutsche Verlags-Anstalt.

Poe, Marshall T. (2011) *A History of Communications: Media and Society from the Evolution of Speech to the Internet*. Cambridge: Cambridge University Press.

Popper, Karl R. (1959) *The Logic of Scientific Discovery*. London: Hutchinson.

Pries, Ludger (2001) *New Transnational Social Spaces: International Migration and Transnational Companies in the Early Twenty-First Century*. London: Routledge.

Quandt, Thorsten, Grüninger, Helmut and Wimmer, Jeffrey (2009) 'The Grey-Haired Gaming Generation: Findings from an Explorative Interview Study on Older Computer Gamers'. *Games and Culture*, 4 (1), pp. 27–46.

Reckwitz, Andreas (2005) 'Kulturelle Differenzen aus praxeologischer Perspektive: Kulturelle Globalisierung jenseits von Modernisierungstheorie und Kulturessentialismus'. In Ilja Srubar, Joachim Renn and Ulrich Wenzel (eds.) *Kulturen vergleichen: Sozial- und kulturwissenschaftliche Grundlagen und Kontroverse*. Wiesbaden: VS, pp. 92–111.

Reichertz, Jo (2008) *Die Macht der Worte und der Medien*. Second edition. Wiesbaden: VS.

References

Reichertz, Jo (2009) *Kommunikationsmacht: Was ist Kommunikation und was vermag sie? Und weshalb vermag sie das?* Wiesbaden: VS.

Reichertz, Jo (2011) 'Communicative Power is Power over Identity'. *Communications*, 36 (2), pp. 147–68.

Rheingold, Howard (1993) 'A Slice of Life in My Virtual Community'. In Linda M. Harasim (ed.) *Global Networks: Computers and International Communication*. Cambridge: Cambridge University Press, pp. 57–80.

Rheingold, Howard (1995) *The Virtual Community: Finding Connection in a Computerized World*. London: Minerva.

Robins, Kevin and Aksoy, Asu (2006) 'Thinking Experience: Transnational Media and Migrants' Minds'. In James Curran and David Morley (eds.) *Media and Cultural Theory*. London and New York: Routledge, pp. 86–99.

Röser, Jutta (ed.) (2007) *MedienAlltag: Domestizierungsprozesse alter und neuer Medien*. Wiesbaden: VS.

Röser, Jutta, Thomas, Tanja and Peil, Corinna (eds.) (2009) *Alltag in den Medien – Medien im Alltag*. Wiesbaden: VS.

Rucht, Dieter (1994) *Modernisierung und neue soziale Bewegungen: Deutschland, Frankreich und USA im Vergleich*. Frankfurt: Campus.

Rusch, Gebhard (2008) 'Mediendynamik: Explorationen zur Theorie des Medienwandel'. *Navigationen*, 7 (1), pp. 13–94.

Sander, Uwe and Vollbrecht, Ralf (1987) 'Aufwachsen und Leben in medialen Umwelten: Ein sozialökologischer Ansatz der Medienforschung'. *Communications*, 13 (2), pp. 121–34.

Saxer, Ulrich (ed.) (1998) *Medien-Kulturkommunikation*. Special Issue of *Publizistik*. Opladen: Westdeutscher Verlag.

Schipper, Bernd (2005) 'Invisible Religion: Religion im öffentlichen Raum'. *Ästhetik & Kommunikation*, 36 (131), pp. 27–32.

Schmidt, Siegfried J. (1992) 'Medien, Kultur: Medienkultur. Ein konstruktivistisches Gesprächsangebot'. In Siegfried J. Schmidt (ed.) *Kognition und Gesellschaft: Der Diskurs des Radikalen Konstruktivismus 2*. Frankfurt: Suhrkamp, pp. 425–50.

Schmidt, Siegfried J. (1994a) 'Die Wirklichkeit des Beobachters'. In Klaus Merten, Siegfried J. Schmidt and Siegfried Weischenberg (eds.) *Die Wirklichkeit der Medien: Eine Einführung in die Kommunikationswissenschaft*. Opladen: Westdeutscher, pp. 3–19.

Schmidt, Siegfried J. (1994b) *Kognitive Autonomie und soziale Orientierung: Konstruktivistische Bemerkungen zum Zusammenhang von Kognition, Kommunikation, Medien und Kultur*. Frankfurt: Suhrkamp.

Schmidt, Siegfried J. (2000) *Kalte Faszination: Medien, Kultur, Wissenschaft in der Mediengesellschaft*. Weilerswist: Velbrück.

Schmidt, Siegfried J. (2003) *Geschichten & Diskurse: Abschied vom Konstruktivismus*. Reinbek b. Hamburg: Rowohlt.

References

Schmidt, Siegfried J. (2008) *Systemflirts: Ausflüge in die Medienkulturgesellschaft.* Weilerswist: Velbrück.

Schmidt, Siegfried J. (2010) *Die Endgültigkeit der Vorläufigkeit: Prozessualität als Argumentationsstrategie.* Weilerswist: Velbrück.

Schofield Clark, L. (2009) 'Theories: Mediatization and Media Ecology'. In Knut Lundby (ed.) *Mediatization: Concept, Changes, Consequences.* New York: Peter Lang, pp. 83–98.

Schröder, Kim Christian (1994) 'Audience Semiotics, Interpretive Communities and the "Ethnographic Turn" in Media Research'. *Media, Culture & Society*, 16 (2), pp. 337–47.

Schrott, Andrea (2009) 'Dimensions: Catch-All Label or Technical Term'. In Knut Lundby (ed.) *Mediatization: Concept, Changes, Consequences.* New York: Peter Lang, pp. 41–61.

Schulz, Winfried (2004) 'Reconstructing Mediatization as an Analytical Concept'. *European Journal of Communication*, 19 (1), pp. 87–101.

Schütz, Alfred (1967) *Phenomenology of the Social World.* New York: Northwestern University Press.

Schütz, Alfred and Luckmann, Thomas (1973) *The Structures of the Life-World.* 2 vols. Evanston, IL: Northwestern University Press.

Shibutani, Tomatsu (1955) 'Reference Groups as Perspectives'. *American Journal of Sociology*, 60 (6), pp. 562–9.

Silver, David (2000) 'Looking Backwards, Looking Forwards: Cyberculture Studies 1990–2000'. In David Gauntlett (ed.) *Web.Studies: Rewiring Media Studies for the Digital Age.* London: Arnold, pp. 19–30.

Silverstone, Roger (1999) *Why Study the Media?* London: Sage.

Silverstone, Roger and Georgiou, Myria (2005) 'Editorial Introduction: Media and Minorities in Multicultural Europe'. *Journal of Ethnic and Migration Studies*, 31, pp. 433–41.

Silverstone, Roger and Hirsch, Eric (eds.) (1992). *Consuming Technologies: Media and Information in Domestic Spaces.* London and New York: Routledge.

Stöber, Rudolf (2003a) *Mediengeschichte: Die Evolution 'neuer' Medien von Gutenberg bis Gates. Eine Einführung. Band 1: Presse – Telekommunikation.* Wiesbaden: Westdeutscher.

Stöber, Rudolf (2003b) *Mediengeschichte: Die Evolution 'neuer' Medien von Gutenberg bis Gates. Eine Einführung. Band 2: Film – Rundfunk – Multimedia.* Wiesbaden: Westdeutscher.

Strauss, Anselm (1978) 'A Social World Perspective'. *Studies in Symbolic Interactionism*, 1 (1), pp. 119–28.

Strauss, Anselm (1993) *Continual Permutations of Action.* New York: de Gruyter.

Strömbäck, Jesper (2008) 'Four Phases of Mediatization: An Analysis of the Mediatization of Politics'. *The International Journal of Press/Politics*, 13 (3), pp. 228–46.

References

Strömbäck, Jesper and Esser, Frank (2009) 'Shaping Politics: Mediatization and Media Environmentalism'. In Knut Lundby (ed.) *Mediatization: Concept, Changes, Consequences*. New York: Peter Lang, pp. 205–23.

Strübing, Jörg (2007) *Anselm Strauss*. Konstanz: UVK.

Tenbruck, Friedrich H. (1972) 'Gesellschaft und Gesellschaften: Gesellschaftstypen'. In Alfred Bellebaum (ed.) *Die moderne Gesellschaft*. Freiburg: Herder, pp. 54–71.

Tepe, Daniel and Hepp, Andreas (2007) 'Digitale Produktionsgemeinschaften: Die Open-Source-Bewegung zwischen kooperativer Softwareherstellung und deterritorialer politischer Vergemeinschaftung'. In Christian Stegbauer and Michael Jäckel (eds.) *Social Software: Formen der Kooperation in computerbasierten Netzwerken*. Wiesbaden: VS, pp. 27–48.

Thomas, Tanja (ed.) (2008) *Medienkultur und soziales Handeln*. Wiesbaden: VS.

Thomas, Tanja (2009) 'Michael Foucault: Diskurs, Macht und Subjekt'. In Andreas Hepp, Friedrich Krotz and Tanja Thomas (eds.) *Schlüsselwerke der Cultural Studies*. Wiesbaden: VS, pp. 58–71.

Thompson, John B. (1995) *The Media and Modernity: A Social Theory of the Media*. Cambridge: Cambridge University Press.

Thussu, Daya Kishan (1998) 'Localizing the Global: Zee TV in India'. In Daya Kishan Thussu (ed.) *Electronic Empires: Global Media and Local Resistance*. London: Arnold, pp. 273–94.

Thussu, Daya Kishan (ed.) (2010) *Internationalizing Media Studies: Impediments and Imperatives*. London: Routledge.

Tölölyan, Khachig (1991) 'The Nation-State and Its Others: In Lieu of a Preface'. *Diaspora*, 1 (1), pp. 3–7.

Tomlinson, John (1999) *Globalization and Culture*. Cambridge: Polity.

Tönnies, Ferdinand (2001) *Community and Civil Society*. Cambridge: Cambridge University Press.

Traub, Hans (1933) *Grundbegriffe des Zeitungswesen*. Stuttgart: Poeschel.

Turkle, Sherry (1995) *Life on the Screen: Identity in the Age of the Internet*. New York: Simon & Schuster.

Ulmer, Bernd and Bergmann, Jörg R. (1993) 'Medienrekonstruktionen als kommunikative Gattungen'. In Werner Holly and Ulrich Püschel (eds.) *Medienrezeption als Aneignung*. Opladen: Westdeutscher, pp. 81–102.

Urry, John (1995) *Consuming Places*. London: Routledge.

Urry, John (2007) *Mobilities*. Cambridge: Polity.

Vowe, Gerhard (2006) 'Mediatisierung der Politik? Ein theoretischer Ansatz auf dem Prüfstand'. *Publizistik*, 51 (4), pp. 437–55.

Wagner, Hans (1998) 'Das Fachstichwort Massenkommunikation'. In Otto Groth, *Vermittelte Mitteilung: Ein journalistisches Modell der Massenkommunikation* (ed. Wolfgang R. Langenbucher). Munich: Fischer, pp. 187–240.

Weber, Max (2013) *Economy and Society. Part I*. Basingstoke: Palgrave Macmillan.

References

Weber, Max (2009) *Wirtschaft und Gesellschaft: Gemeinschaften. Studienausgabe der Max Weber Gesamtausgabe Band I/22-1*. Tübingen: Mohr.

Welsch, Wolfgang (1999) 'Transculturality – The Changing Forms of Cultures Today'. In Bundesminister für Wissenschaft und Verkehr & Internationales Forschungszentrum für Kulturwissenschaften (ed.) *The Contemporary Study of Culture*. Vienna: Turia & Kant, pp. 217–44.

Williams, Raymond (2003) *Television: Technology and Cultural Form*. London and New York: Routledge.

Winter, Carsten (1996) *Predigen unter freiem Himmel: Die medienkulturellen Funktionen der Bettelmönche und ihr geschichtlicher Hintergrund*. Bardowick: Wissenschaftler Verlag.

Wittel, Andreas (2008) 'Towards a Network Sociality'. In Andreas Hepp, Friedrich Krotz, Shaun Moores and Carsten Winter (eds.) *Connectivity, Network and Flow: Conceptualizing Contemporary Communications*. Cresskill, NJ: Hampton Press, pp. 157–82.

Woodward, Kathryn (1997) 'Concepts of Identity and Difference'. In Kathryn Woodward (ed.) *Identity and Difference*. London: Sage, pp. 7–50.

Index

Index

communitization
  concept/definitions 100–2
  debates on 98–100
  deterritorialized 113–21
  locality/translocality 102–8
  mediatized subjective horizons 121–6
  paradox of 102
  territorialization/deterritorialization
    108–12
  traditional/post-traditional 100–2
  transformation/loss 100
connectivity theory 14–15, 83–4
convergence culture 26
Couldry, Nick 32, 37, 43, 44, 133, 134–5
Critical Theory 10
cultural history as sequence 12–15
cultural identity 125–6
culture
  concept 4–5
  and construction of reality 19
  entrepreneurial 27
  as functional organism 72
  as programme 19–20–20
  as system 19
culture industry
  commodities produced by 8–9
  and omnipresence of media culture 9–11
  and standardization 9
cultures of mediatization
  analysing patterns 136–8
  approach to 6
  biological connection 22
  communicative figurations 92–7
  concept 69–75
  as constitutive of reality 17–23
  critical stance 143
  decentring 132–6
  developing theories 128–32
  four-phase development 14
  globalization of communication 74–5
  as hybrid 72
  as marked by the medium 11–17
  as mediatization of culture 29
  mediatized worlds 75–83
  misconceptions concerning 7
  network sociality 91–2
  networks of communication 83–91
  as omnipresent 8–11
  prospect for 142–4
  reason for writing about/dealing with
    1–2
  review of theory/analysis 6
  as technologized 23–8
  thickening 72, 73, 74, 75

transcultural comparisons 138–41
translocal 71–3
cyberculture
  concept 23–4
  and convergence culture 26
  critical studies 25
  and culture of production 27–8
  popular 24
  studies 24
  utopianism of 24, 25–6, 27

decentring 132–3
  concept 135
  individual medium 134
  media-centrism 135–6
  and mediated centres 133–4
  social centre 134–5
deterritorial translocal communitization 111
  communicative networks 114
  deterritorialized extension 113
  ethnic aspects 114–15
  networks of local groups 113
  political aspects 116–17
  religious 118–21
  thematic aspects 115–16
  translocal horizon of meanings 113
  see also territorialization/
    deterritorialization
diasporas 94–7, 109, 111–12, 114–15,
  121, 125
discourse analysis 137
Dovey, Jon 24
Durkheim, Émile 50

Elias, Norbert 51, 92–3
entrepreneurial culture 27

Facebook 63, 135
falsification principle 48–9
Faulstich, Werner 21
Fiore, Quentin *see* McLuhan, Marshall and
  Quentin Fiore
first-order media 4
form of identity 126
Fornäs, Johan 37
Foucault, Michel 77
Frankfurt School 8–10
Friesen, Norm 16

García Canclini, Néstor 75
Gauntlett, David
  Making is Connecting 25–6
  Web.Studies 24, 25
Gibson, William, *Neuromancer* 23

163

Index

Index

media reference 107
mediatic turn 16
mediation
  by the media 106–7
  and communication 33–6
  cultural necessity for 33
  distinguished from mediatization 31–8
  important/necessary 32–3, 37–8
  as open-ended process 36–7
  and television 34–5
mediatization 6
  concept 29, 69
  constructive process of cultural
    articulation 143
  cultural patterns/questions of power
    144
  and development of modernity 29–31
  direct 43
  distinguished from mediation 31–8
  indirect 43
  logic(s) 38–46
  and media-centrism 134–6
  as metaprocess 46–54
  multiperspectival critique 144
  over time 53
  as panorama 50–4
  prospect for 142–4
  qualitative aspects 54
  quantitative aspects 52–4
  regarding space 53
  social dimension 53–4
mediatized migrants 94–7
mediatized worlds
  and arenas 81
  changing 82
  communicative 79–80, 81, 82
  concept/definitions 76
  interlocking 82
  scale 82
  social world perspective 80–1
  structures of the life-world 76–8
  subjective standpoint 79
  symbolic interactionism 79
medium, concept of 3–4
Medium Theory 60, 74, 75, 106
  ambivalence towards 16
  development of 11–12
  electronic media 13
  as inadequate 16–17
  link with ideal types of society 14–15
  macro approaches 12–14
  overestimations of 17
  print culture 13
metaprocess 47–51, 52, 69

Meyrowitz, Joshua 11–12, 14
  No Sense of Place 12
migrant communities 94–7
modern print culture 13
modern societies 15
modernity 29–31
Monaco, James 39
Mondo magazine 24
Morley, David 76, 132–3
Morris, Merrill 88–9
moulding forces of the media 90, 97, 127
  approaches 55–7
  concept 54–5
  as convergence of institutionalization/
    reification of communicative action
    57–64
  systematization of communication 64–8
  technology/cultural form 55–6

Nederveen Pieterse, Jan 71–2
network sociality 91–2, 99–100
networks 57, 90–1
  see also communication network
New Economy 91, 92, 100
newspapers 32–3
Niederbacher, Arne 130
nodes 84–5, 87
non-mediacentric media studies 132–3

objectification 58
Occupy movement 111
Ogan, Christine 88–9
Ong, Walter, *Orality and Literacy* 13
Open Source movement 27
oral society 12, 15

panorama 49–51, 52, 69, 131
pattern analysis 136–8
physical deterritorialization 108, 109
political campaigns 16–17
Popper, Karl, *The Logic of Scientific
    Discovery* 48
power 62–3, 144
primary culture 5
project identities 117

radical constructivism 17–23
Reichertz, Jo 62, 63
reification 58–9
religious communitization 111, 118–21
  Catholic Church 118–19
  fundamentalist movements 120
  Marian apparitions 120
  New Age movements 119

Index